DISTANCE IN PREACHING

ID0920755

Distance in Preaching

Room to Speak, Space to Listen

Michael Brothers

WILLIAM B. EERDMANS PUBLISHING COMPANY

GRAND RAPIDS, MICHIGAN / CAMBRIDGE, U.K.

© 2014 Michael Brothers
All rights reserved

Wm. B. Eerdmans Publishing Co.
2140 Oak Industrial Drive N.E., Grand Rapids, Michigan 49505 /
P.O. Box 163, Cambridge CB3 9PU U.K.

Printed in the United States of America

20 19 18 17 16 15 14   7 6 5 4 3 2 1

Library of Congress Cataloging-in-Publication Data

Brothers, Michael.
Distance in preaching: room to speak, space to listen / Michael Brothers.
pages   cm
Includes bibliographical references and index.
ISBN 978-0-8028-6969-2 (pbk.: alk. paper)
1. Preaching. 2. Listening — Religious aspects — Christianity.   I. Title.

BV4211.3.B759   2014
251 — dc23

2014002439

www.eerdmans.com

To Lauren,
who draws me near,
and gives me room to be free.

Contents

1. Setting the Stage   1

   A Change in Hearing   1

   Proposal and Plan of the Book   3

   Introducing Distance in Preaching   6

2. Aesthetic Distance in Performance   11

   Aesthetic Distance   11

   Performing Distance   22

   Backdrop for Preaching   45

3. Distance in Preaching: Fred Craddock's Homiletical Method   47

   Preserving the Text: Distance in Interpretation   48

   Protecting the Hearer: Distance in the Sermon   66

   Respecting the Hearer: Distance in Delivery   79

   Summary   87

4. Absorption in the Sermon: Postliberal Homiletics   88

   Mark Ellingsen's Homiletic   90

   Charles Campbell's Homiletic   112

   Absorption Reconsidered   131

5. Clearing the Sanctuary: Room and Space   137

   Distance Reconsidered   137

   Recent Proposals   140

   Conclusion   146

   Two Sermons

   Were You There? A Sermon on John 19:16b-25   148

   Sibling Revelry: A Sermon on Luke 15:11-32   153

   BIBLIOGRAPHY   158

   INDEX   175

CHAPTER ONE

Setting the Stage

A Change in Hearing

"I feel crowded." This was the response by a young woman to a sermon zealously preached in my recent seminary course entitled "Preaching the Sermon." Her comment was not an unusual one; similar sermon responses throughout the term included these:

"I felt emotionally manipulated."
"I don't like it when preachers say, 'Now I know what you're thinking. . . .' You don't know what I'm thinking!"
"*You* were into the [biblical] story, but *I* really don't know it."
"There was no place for a differing opinion."
"Let me make my own decisions."
"It was too much; I had to tune you out."
"The bigger you got, the smaller I felt."
"I kept backing up, but you kept moving forward."

One student's astute critique expressed the overall ethos of classroom listening: "There was no room for me in the sermon." This ethos can be described as *distance.*

Distance in preaching can be described as a "psychic" separation, holding hearers "at bay," keeping them from "direct participation" in a biblical text via the sermon's form, technique, style, and delivery. Distance can be contrasted with "nearness," or "participation," which draws the hearer into the sermon. This functional definition of distance involves the psychic, aesthetic, spatial, and critical relationship between the sermon and the hearer. Distance in the sermon is created by the posture of the hearer, the structure and content of the sermon, the form, content, and style of the biblical text, and the role of the preacher with respect to individual hearers and the community.

In the last decade I have noticed a dramatic change in how sermons are listened to and heard in the classroom. Much of this shift can be described as a change of *distance* between the hearers and the sermon, between the hearers and the preacher, and between the hearers and the biblical text. My interest in distance in preaching arose from classroom settings toward the end of the last century. Having taught preaching and speech performance in both seminary and university settings, I was curious about the dramatic differences between the seminarians' discussions of distance and those of university students. In the preaching classroom in seminary, student responses to sermons went like this: "You had me until the part. . . ." "You seemed distant." "Reach out and talk to us." "You never talked to me directly." "I felt separated from you." "Convince me!" "Draw me in." "I want you to overwhelm me!" By contrast, responses to performances of literature in speech performance classrooms at the university went like this: "You were too close for comfort; you forced me to back away." "You overpowered the poem with your voice and gestures." "Let the piece speak for itself." "Don't complete the story for us; let us do that ourselves."[1] In both the university and seminary settings, students viewed the listeners' *participation* as a positive element in the presentations by their peers, and they encouraged its use through elements of style and delivery. In a striking contrast, students of speech performance considered distance a necessary component of performance, something that allowed the audience to experience the *work* and not just the *performer*, whereas seminarians

1. The classroom experiences to which I refer were at Princeton Theological Seminary, Eastern Baptist Theological Seminary, University of South Florida, and The School of Communication, Northwestern University.

considered distance an obstacle between the preacher and the congregation — something that kept hearers from "drawing close to God's Word."

In recent years I have become aware of a change in sermon responses
in courses that emphasize both sermon construction and preaching "live"
in front of the class. Comments expressing a desire to be drawn in, con-
vinced, and overwhelmed have all but disappeared. Taking their place are
requests calling for "room" in the preached sermon for the hearers' own
interpretations and experiences, and calling for a respect for the distance,
or "space," within which hearers can have their own responses and make
their own decisions.

This change in the hearers' response to preaching, and the differences
between the contexts of preaching and speech performance, prompted
me to investigate in this book *distance* in the disciplines of aesthetics, performance studies, and homiletics. My aim is to contribute to a greater
understanding of distance in the field of homiletics; equip teachers and
students of preaching to return to the classroom with an informed ability
to evaluate its function in sermon form, style, and delivery; and encourage
preachers to acquire greater understanding and skill in the use of distance
as they create and preach sermons. My hope is that this understanding,
combined with ability, may provide today's preacher with *room* to speak
the gospel, and may provide today's hearer with *space* within which to
hear the gospel.

Proposal and Plan of the Book

In this book I propose that distance as a hermeneutical tool and a dynamic
in communication is vital to today's hearing of the gospel and thus should
be intentionally used in sermon form, style, and delivery. In placing Fred
Craddock's sermon method into conversation with speech performance
studies, critical challenges made by postliberal homiletics, and more recent homiletical proposals by David Buttrick, Charles Bartow, and Jana
Childers, I evaluate the "benefits of distance" for the message and the
hearer in today's preaching.

After clarifying terms, I use the remainder of chapter 1 to describe
Fred Craddock's introduction of distance into the field of homiletics in his

lectures at Yale Divinity School in 1978. In chapter 2, I explore aesthetic distance as a concept and dynamic in philosophy, speech performance, theater, and literary criticism. I trace distance from its beginnings as a universal aesthetic principle to its current understanding as a dynamic device in performance, rituals, and literature.

Against the backdrop of aesthetics, performance, and literature, chapter 3 discusses Craddock's proposal that distance protects the integrity of the biblical text and preserves the dignity of the hearer. I argue that Craddock's intentional use of distance is not a pragmatic pandering to the hearer, but is theologically warranted and morally justified with regard to the hearer and sermon style. Using excerpts from Craddock's published sermons, and transcriptions from selected audio and video recordings, I analyze Craddock's use of "distancing devices" in style and delivery that allow "room" for "free participation" and a "new hearing" of the gospel.

In chapter 4, I discuss Mark Ellingsen's and Charles Campbell's respective postliberal homiletics, which provide a sharp contrast to Craddock's understanding of distance. Although both Ellingsen and Campbell claim the "postliberal" label, I note their distinctively different uses of Hans Frei and George Lindbeck as a basis for their homiletical proposals. I then evaluate "absorption" in their respective sermon methods and models in light of the concept of distance — both in performance theory and in Craddock's homiletical theory.

Chapter 5 concludes with a reevaluation of distance in light of postliberal challenges regarding the *experience* of the hearer and the change in hearers within the last thirty-five years. I end by offering two of my sermons as illustrations of distancing, hoping to provide room for the biblical text and space for the hearers' response.

Terms

I describe *distance* throughout this project according to the varied understandings and uses of particular authors. Terms that are unique to particular writers — for example, "overhearing," "indirect address," "intratextuality," and "ascriptive logic" — I define with respect to their specific proposals. Because of the interdisciplinary nature of this project, readers should be aware that terms have different meanings and uses in their respective fields. For clarity, I offer the following definitions of selected terms:

Sermon Webster's dictionary defines *sermon* as "a religious discourse delivered in public" usually by clergy "as a part of a worship service."[2] In this project, the components of a sermon may include a biblical text, gospel message, the Holy Spirit, sermon text, manuscript, preacher, hearer, congregation, and context, depending on the homiletician being discussed. Webster's second definition is "a written discourse delivered or intended for delivery of a sermon." I will often refer to this second meaning of "sermon" as *sermon text*. I will use both of these meanings of sermon throughout this project.

Performance In *Performance: Texts and Contexts*, Carol Simpson Stern and Bruce Henderson describe performance as "a human activity, interactional in nature and involving symbolic forms and live bodies, which constitutes meaning, expression or affirming individual and cultural values." They note Victor Turner's tracing of the term to the Old French *perfournir*, meaning "to complete" or "to carry out thoroughly."[3] In its broadest sense, I will use "performance" in this project according to the Stern and Henderson description. When referring to the performance of a sermon or the performance of literature, I will use Webster's first definition ("the act or process of carrying out something") and the second definition ("a public presentation") and Stern and Henderson's description of the performance event ("the embodiment or enactment of the text").

Text Webster's dictionary provides three meanings of "text" that I will use in this project: "the original or printed words and form of a literary work"; "a verse or passage of Scripture chosen especially for the subject of a sermon"; and "the form and substance of something written or spoken."

2. All dictionary definitions are from *Webster's Third New International Unabridged Dictionary* (Chicago: Encyclopedia Britannica, 2002), noted as *Webster's* dictionary or simply *Webster's*.

3. Carol Simpson Stern and Bruce Henderson, *Performance: Texts and Contexts* (White Plains, NY: Longman Publishing, 1993), p. 546.

Pertinent to sermons that are preached without the creation or use of a manuscript, Stern and Henderson note that a text "may be oral, written, gestural, or some combination of these, is repeatable and capable of having invisible boundaries placed around it, separating it from other external features."[4]

Sermon Text In this book I will refer to *sermon text* as an artifact that has been written, recorded on audio- or videocassettes, or transcribed.

Oral Interpretation and Interpretation For the purposes of this project, we can describe *oral interpretation* as a practice and discipline and as "the interpretation of literature through the medium of performance." Although the discipline became known as simply *interpretation*, I will use its former title ("oral interpretation") to distinguish it from interpretation in biblical studies and hermeneutics.

Performance Studies Stern and Henderson note that performance refers to continuums of human activity, "from individual role playing in everyday life to collective staged performances; from everyday life performances to artificial, stylized performances (such as plays); and from ordinary performances to extraordinary performances or from personal narrative to ecstatic trance. Performance embraces cultural and literary performance as well as performance art, which includes a variety of activity from aesthetic to political, individual to collective."[5] For the purpose of this project, I will use the term "performance studies" as it pertains to the study of the performance of texts and rituals.

Introducing Distance in Preaching

Thirty-five years ago, Fred Craddock took the podium as the Lyman Beecher lecturer for 1978 at Yale Divinity School. In his series of lectures, entitled "Overhearing the Gospel: The Illusion of Truth without Imag-

---

4. Stern and Henderson, *Performance*, p. 547.
5. Stern and Henderson, *Performance*, p. 546.

ination," he formally introduced the concept of distance to the field of homiletics.[6] Eclectically drawing on works by various authors, including philosophers Søren Kierkegaard and Paul Ricoeur, writers George Eliot and Thomas de Quincey, and representatives of the New Hermeneutic such as Robert Funk and Amos Wilder, Craddock created his proposal of distance as a function of "overhearing" Scripture, the sermon, and the gospel. In his final lecture, he summarizes his proposal:

> The modest proposal being offered here is that the listener's experience of *overhearing* is a natural, effective, and at times life-changing dynamic that belongs in the church's classroom and sanctuary. And since it is also appropriate to the study, the transition from desk to pulpit or lectern is made less awkward and difficult. (p. 120; italics added)

Craddock's proposal of "overhearing" begins and ends with a concern for the hearer. In defense of this concern, he says:

> The Christian tradition, biblical and extra-biblical, came to us from those who *heard* it, and we *hear* it and pass it on to other *hearers*. The stamp of listening and the listenability of the message is on it when we get it, and in telling it, we confirm that it is listenable. To give such attention to the listener is not a concession to "what they want to hear," playing to the balcony or to the groundlings, nor is it an introduction to how to succeed as a speaker; it is no more or less than to describe the shape of the subject matter (it came from the listeners) and the nature of the occasion (to effect a hearing). (p. 121)

Having established the experience of *listening* as "the governing consideration" in the communicative event of preaching that "harnesses the imaginative, emotive, and cognitive powers" of the preacher, Craddock characterizes the "posture" of listening, called "overhearing," as made up

6. Fred B. Craddock, "Overhearing the Gospel: The Illusion of Truth without Imagination," Lyman Beecher Lectures, Yale Divinity School, New Haven, Connecticut, 1978; published as *Overhearing the Gospel: Preaching and Teaching the Faith to Persons Who Have Heard It All Before* (Nashville: Abingdon, 1978). Hereafter, page references to this latter publication appear in parentheses in the text.

of two elements: distance and participation. Craddock describes the "benefits of distance" as twofold. The first function of distance in the sermon is that it preserves the "invaluable benefits" of the message.

> For the message, distance preserves its objectivity as history, its continuity as tradition, and its integrity as a word that has existence prior to and apart from the individual listener. In other words, the distance between the message and the listener conveys the sense of the substantive nature and independence of the message, qualities that add to rather than detract from the persuasive and attention-drawing power of the message. . . . This I am calling distance, a necessary dimension of the experience of overhearing that says to the listener, "You are sitting in on something that is of such significance that it could have gone on without you." (pp. 121-22)

Whereas the first benefit of distance is the protection of the message, the second is a concern for the listener. Craddock continues:

> As for the benefit distance provides the listener, we have talked of the room the listener has, room in which to reflect, accept, reject, decide. As a listener, I must have that freedom, all the more so if the matter before me is of ultimate importance. (p. 122)

After describing the benefits that distance provides for the message and listener, Craddock concludes:

> The other element in the experience of overhearing is participation: free participation on the part of the hearer in the issues, the crises, the decision, the judgment, and the promise of the message. Participation means the listener overcomes the distance, not because the speaker "applied" everything, but because the listener identified with experiences and thoughts related in the message that were analogous to his own. . . . [T]he speaker who wants the listeners to overhear will preserve distance in narration, but the vocabulary, idiom, imagery, and descriptive detail will be such as will allow points or moments in the process at which the listener can "enter," identify, be enrolled. (p. 123)

8

In Craddock's proposal, the counterpart of distance is also its goal: "free participation" on the part of the hearer. Craddock's proposal ends where it began, a concern for the hearer.

To the audience at Yale Divinity School, Craddock introduced distance in preaching as an approach to a biblical text, as dynamics within particular biblical texts, and as intentional tactics in the creation, presentation, and delivery of a sermon. Across campus from where Craddock was speaking, in the Yale Repertory Theater's archives, were the playbills from its American premiere of Bertolt Brecht's *The Little Mahagonny*. Eight years before Craddock proposed distance as an intentional separation of the congregation from the sermon, Brecht's signature use of distancing through "alienation devices" pushed audience members away from emotional identifications with characters in order to see the play's greater significance for social change.[7] (A decade later, homiletician David Buttrick would credit Brecht with having informed his use of distance in sermon moves and structures in order to address the changing consciousness of the hearer.) Nearby, housed in Yale's Beinecke Rare Book and Manuscript Library, were scene and set designs for *Our Town* by Thornton Wilder (1879-1975). In these sketches, an almost bare theater stage reflects a vision of providing "room for the audience's imagination" through the removal of "obtrusive bric-a-brac."[8] In his lectures, Craddock quotes Wilder as he encourages preachers to make "room" for the imagination instead of overcrowding sermons with too much description. And while Craddock was describing the hearers' experience of distance in preaching as similar to that of an audience for a concert or play, across campus, shelved in Yale's Sterling Memorial Library under "aesthetics," was Edward Bullough's seminal article entitled "'Psychical Distance' as a Factor in Art and an Aesthetic Principle." Originally published in *The British Journal of Psychology* in 1912, that essay introduced the concept of "psychical distance," which became a defining

---

7. Yale University, Yale Repertory Theatre: http://www.yale.edu (accessed February 2012).

8. Thornton Wilder, preface to *Three Plays by Thornton Wilder: Our Town, The Skin of Our Teeth, The Matchmaker* (New York: Bantam Books, 1961), p. xi; Thornton Wilder Society: http://www.thorntonwildersociety.com (accessed February 2012); Yale University, Beinecke Rare Book and Manuscript Library: http://www.yale.edu (accessed February 2012).

factor for the discussion of "aesthetic attitude" and "aesthetic experience" in philosophy, and of "aesthetic dynamics" between the work and audience in theater, music, literature, and the visual arts.[9] Although Craddock's proposal of distance may have been new to his homiletical audience, writers in the areas of philosophy, the performing arts, and literature were well acquainted with its use. It is to these disciplines that we now turn.

---

9. Edward Bullough, "'Psychical Distance' as a Factor in Art and an Aesthetic Principle," *The British Journal of Psychology* 5 (June 1912): 87-118; reprinted in Bullough, *Aesthetics: Lectures and Essays* (Stanford: Stanford University Press, 1957); Orbis, Yale University Library Catalog: http://www.yale.edu (accessed February 2012).

CHAPTER TWO

Aesthetic Distance in Performance

Aesthetic Distance

Distance in homiletics has its roots in aesthetics and speech performance. Noël Carroll delineates three helpful uses of the term "aesthetics." The first is "aesthetics" in its broadest sense, roughly equivalent to "philosophy of art." Carroll notes that even among philosophers the two terms are frequently interchangeable. A second, narrower use of the term refers to the artistic properties of a work of art or a performance. These properties may be identified as expressive: for example, the artwork was "unified," "graceful," "elegant," or "brittle." We might use anthropomorphic terminology, such as "sad" or "somber." Although these properties are considered part of the work itself, they are still response-dependent because they are ascribed to the hearer or viewer.[1]

It is the third use of the term that pertains to distance. Here "aesthetics" derives its meaning from the Greek word *aisthēsis*, which includes "sense perception," or "sensory cognition," in its definition. In the middle of the eighteenth century, theorist Alexander Gottlieb Baumgarten (1714-1762) first used the name for the modern discipline of "aesthetics" in his dissertation "Philosophical Reflections on some matters pertaining to Poetry." Here Baumgarten describes "aesthetics," the philosophical

---

1. Noël Carroll, *Philosophy of Art: A Contemporary Introduction* (New York: Routledge, Taylor, and Francis Group, 2002), pp. 156, 157.

study of art, as "sense perception." By emphasizing the senses, Baumgarten and other theorists who followed him made a significant shift from the philosophy of art in general toward the "addressed spectators" and their "reception" of the work. Whereas aesthetics as the philosophy of art is "object-oriented," *aesthetic* as response-dependent or sense perception is "reception-oriented."[2]

In this third sense, "aesthetic" is often used as an adjective, such as "aesthetic experience," "aesthetic perception," "aesthetic attitude," or "aesthetic distance." When philosophers or theorists use "aesthetic" as a modifier, they signal intent in the interaction between the artwork and reader, listener, and viewer. In this sense, "aesthetic attitude" as a part of an "aesthetic experience" describes commonly recurring responses to art and performance. Approached with an aesthetic attitude, an aesthetic object has the function of being the proper locus of appreciation and criticism (criticism understood to include description, interpretation, and evaluation). The concept of an aesthetic object has a "normative function," for it is supposed to guide our attention to the qualities of art and nature that are "aesthetically relevant" — and thereby serve as a foundation for criticism.[3]

As a form of aesthetic experience, "aesthetic distance" is a particular kind of recurring response to performance involving the artwork and the perceiver. As part of an aesthetic attitude, aesthetic distance can be described as responses that occur when people distance themselves from an object they perceive, suspend their desires and other feelings, and are left with the mere experience of contemplating it.[4]

2. Carroll, *Philosophy of Art*, pp. 156-59; Ted Cohen and Paul Guyer, "Introduction to Kant's Aesthetics: From Essays in Kant's Aesthetics," in George Dickie, Richard Sclafani, and Ronald Roblin, eds., *Aesthetics: A Critical Anthology* (New York: St. Martin's Press, 1989), 306-7.

3. Carroll, *Philosophy of Art*, pp. 157-59, 202; George Dickie, *Aesthetics* (New York: Bobbs-Merrill, 1971), p. 60. For a further discussion of "aesthetic attitude" and "aesthetic experience," see Jerome Stolnitz, *Aesthetics and Philosophy of Art Criticism: A Critical Introduction* (Boston: Houghton Mifflin, 1960), pp. 34-83.

4. Christopher Janaway, "'Aesthetic Attitude' and 'Aesthetic Distance,'" in Ted Honderich, ed., *The Oxford Companion to Philosophy* (Oxford: Oxford University Press, 1995).

Psychical Distance

Long before the terms "distance" or "aesthetic distance" were coined, scholars and philosophers were discussing forms of distance and aesthetic distance. Perhaps the greatest figure in the interpretation of the beholder's response in art was Immanuel Kant (1728-1804). His work *Critique of Judgment* (1790) greatly influenced a modern understanding of aesthetic experience by analyzing the contemplation of an aesthetic object as being "disinterested."[5] Kant divides his discussion of a theory of beauty, "Analytic of the Beautiful," into four parts, each of which covers a major concept: disinterestedness, universality, the form of purpose, and necessity. George Dickie concisely summarizes the components of Kant's theory in a sentence: "A judgment of beauty is a disinterested, universal and necessary judgment concerning the pleasure which everyone ought to derive from the experience of form."[6]

Under the heading "The Liking That Determines a Judgment of Taste is Devoid of All Interest," Kant discusses disinterestedness: "Everyone has to admit that if a judgment about beauty is mingled with the least interest then it is very partial and not a pure judgment of taste. In order to play the judge in matters of taste, we must not be in the least biased in favor of the thing's existence but must be wholly indifferent about it."[7] Kant continues by explaining "indifference" as a "pure disinterested liking that occurs in a judgment of taste." According to M. H. Abrams, Kant's understanding of disinterested contemplation is where the experience of the art object is independent of one's personal interests and desires, and free from reference to the object's reality, moral effect, or utility.[8] For Kant, fine art was

5. Immanuel Kant, *The Critique of Judgment*, trans. Werner S. Pluhar (Indianapolis: Hackett Publishing, 1987), pp. 43-46 (originally published in Prussia in 1790).

6. Dickie et al., *Aesthetics*, p. 27.

7. Kant, *Critique of Judgment*, p. 46.

8. M. H. Abrams, *A Glossary of Literary Terms* (Fort Worth: Harcourt Brace, 1999), pp. 68-69. For further discussion regarding Kant's aesthetic of "indifference" and "disinterested contemplation," see Gordon Graham, *The Re-enchantment of the World: Art Versus Religion* (New York: Oxford University Press, 2007), p. 23; Henry E. Allison, *Kant's Theory of Taste: A Reading of the Critique of Aesthetic Judgment* (Cambridge: Cambridge University Press, 2001), pp. 85-97; and Cohen and Guyer, "Introduction to Kant's Aesthetics," pp. 306-14.

a free creation of beauty with its own intrinsic value and worth. Through disinterested contemplation, people could enjoy beauty and design simply for their own sake.

Influenced by Kant's understanding of "disinterested contemplation," Edward Bullough (1880-1934) was the first in the twentieth century to formulate the term "Distance" as an aesthetic response to a work of art.[9] His seminal article "'Psychical Distance' as a Factor in Art and an Aesthetic Principle," originally published in 1912 in the *British Journal of Psychology*, has been reprinted extensively and discussed widely in most twentieth-century and contemporary compilations of aesthetic criticism.[10] His influence in introducing "Distance" as a defining factor in aesthetic attitude and aesthetic experience cannot be overestimated. As Susanne Langer says in *Feeling and Form*, Bullough's article is "deservedly famous."[11] Even George Dickie, one of Bullough's harshest critics, claims that the article "has almost become an article of faith for much present-day aesthetic theory."[12]

A professor of Italian at Cambridge University, Edward Bullough relied on his encyclopedic background in the arts and sciences, as well as his personal experience with theater, music, painting, sculpture, and architecture, to characterize a mental process necessary for experiencing art. Bullough noted a "dual attachment" in the perception of art that involved the interplay between "devotion" and a kind of "detachment impossible to obtain, performed for the sake of further ends of ulterior reason" (p. 67).[13] This simultaneous attachment and detachment, separation and involvement, Bullough labels "Distance." He declares: "Distance . . . is obtained

9. When referring to Bullough's work, I will follow his use of the uppercase *D* for the aesthetic concept of "Distance," in contrast to the lowercase *d* for "distancing devices."

10. Edward Bullough, "'Psychical Distance' as a Factor in Art and an Aesthetic Principle," *The British Journal of Psychology* 5 (June 1912): 87-118, reprinted in Bullough, *Aesthetics: Lectures and Essays* (Stanford: Stanford University Press, 1957). Hereafter, page references to this latter work appear in parentheses in the text.

11. Susanne K. Langer, *Feeling and Form* (New York: Scribner, 1953), p. 318.

12. Dickie et al., *Aesthetics*, p. 47.

13. This is also noted in Beverly Whitaker Long, "A 'Distanced' Art: Interpretation at Mid-Century," in David W. Thompson, ed., *Performance of Literature in Historical Perspectives* (Lanham, MD: University Press of America, 1983), pp. 567-87.

by separating the object and its appeal from one's own self by putting it out of gear with practical needs and ends" (p. 96).

Bullough begins his article by differentiating the concept of Distance from other forms of distancing devices in connection with a work of art. "Spatial distance" is literally the measurable space between the "spectator" (Bullough's term) and the work of art. "Represented spatial distance" is distance portrayed or represented in the work itself, for example, a painting of a tree that is portrayed at a distance on the horizon. In painting, this form of distance involves "perspective." A third and more metaphorical form is "temporal distance," which involves the remoteness of art from us in a particular point of time. Whereas all of these forms of distance, whether of space or time, may enhance simultaneous separation and involvement, they derive any aesthetic qualities they possess from "Distance" understood in its broadest connotation, which Bullough calls "Psychical Distance" (pp. 93-94).

As an example of psychical Distance, Bullough surprisingly uses an illustration from nature instead of art. He asks us to imagine a fog at sea. For most, such a natural phenomenon would be an experience of acute unpleasantness, producing feelings of anxiety and fear, straining our sight and hearing for dangerous objects and audible warnings. Its silence and gentleness makes the fog all the more terrifying. The expectant, tacit anxiety and nervousness associated with this experience is what makes fog a dreaded "terror of the sea" (pp. 93-94).

Bullough then observes that at the same time sea fog can be an intense source of relish and enjoyment. By momentarily abstracting from the experience (what phenomenologists would call "bracketing out") its danger and practical unpleasantness, we can now look at the phenomenon "objectively," focusing on and appreciating the features that make up sea fog: its milklike opaqueness, the creamy smoothness of the water, "hypocritically denying," as it were, any suggestion of danger (p. 94). The result is a "concentrated poignancy and delight" that momentarily switches on to contrast sharply with the "blind and distempered anxiety" of fog's other aspects. Like watching some impending catastrophe with the unconcern of a spectator, our "practical interests" snap like a wire from pure "overtension" (p. 94).

This immediate and momentary change of outlook is due to what

Bullough calls the "insertion" of Distance between our "own self" and the self's "affections." Bullough uses the term "affections" in its broadest sense as anything that affects our being. Thus sea fog becomes an illustration of how Distance is produced when apprehending nature or art by putting the phenomenon "out of gear" with the "practical, actual self." Whether in fog, in a painting, or in a play, Distance occurs "by allowing [the self] to stand outside the context of our personal needs and ends — in short, by looking at it 'objectively,' as it has often been called, by permitting only such reactions on our part as emphasize the 'objective' feature of the experience, and by interpreting even our 'subjective' affections not as modes of *our* being but rather as characteristics of the phenomenon." Paradoxically, Bullough's search for what made art appear close and intense led him to Distance (p. 95).[14]

The distanced view of things cannot be our "normal" outlook, since it comes to us as a view of things from their reverse, usually unnoticed, side. Bullough proposes that Distance, therefore, has a "negative, inhibitory aspect" that cuts out the practical side of things and our practical attitude toward them. Simultaneously, Distance has a "positive side" by providing an experience of the new based on Distance's inhibitory action. For Bullough, this experience of the new that comes upon us as a revelation is a factor of all art, "for distance, once it has occurred, can be aesthetically appreciated" (p. 95).

The heart of Bullough's aesthetic is that Distance comes between our own self and its affections, whereby we can experience in a new way the work of art or performance. Bullough says: "Distance, as I said before, is obtained by separating the object and its appeal from one's own self, by putting it out of gear with practical needs and ends. Thereby the 'contemplating' of the object becomes alone possible" (p. 96). Bullough goes on to say that this relationship between the self and the object may be broken, but not to the extent of being "impersonal." For Bullough, Distance is not an impersonal, objective, or purely intellectual exercise; it describes a "personal relation" that is "highly emotionally coloured." What is peculiar to the character of Distance, Bullough says, is that the personal character of the relation has been filtered, "cleaned of the practical concrete nature

14. See also Long, "A 'Distanced' Art," p. 568.

of its appeal without, however, losing its original constitution" (p. 97). Bullough gives as an example our attitude toward the events and characters in a drama: "They appeal to us like persons and incidents of normal experience, except that the side of this appeal, which would usually affect us in a directly personal manner, is held in abeyance. The difference, so well known to us as to be almost trivial, is generally explained by reference to the knowledge that the characters and situations are 'unreal' imaginings" (pp. 97-98).[15]

Here Bullough notes an important paradox. One would think that Distance, by changing our perception and relationship to characters onstage, would render them as "fictitious," thereby altering our feelings toward them. However, he goes on to observe that, paradoxically, the opposite is true: "Distance, which primarily gives to the action the appearance of unreality and not vice versa, is the observation that the same filtration of our sentiments and the same seeming unreality of *actual* men and things occur, when at times, by a sudden change of inward perspective, we are overcome by the feeling that 'all the world's a stage'" (p. 98). This personal but distant relationship is what Bullough calls "the antinomy of Distance" (p. 99).[16]

For Bullough, Distance is a psychological state that can either be achieved or lost. Distance can be lost through "underdistancing" or "overdistancing": "The consequence of a loss of distance through one or other cause is familiar: the verdict in the case of underdistancing is that the work is 'crudely naturalistic,' 'harrowing,' repulsive in its 'realism.' An excess of Distance produces the impression of improbability, artificiality, emptiness or absurdity" (p. 101). The percipient may experience a response to an "underdistanced" performance as discomfort, fear, uneasiness, embarrassment, whereas the response to an "overdistanced" performance may take the form of apathy or incredulity.[17]

---

15. Bullough's understanding of Distance to be holding "in abeyance" the personal aspect of a character in a drama opened the door to twentieth-century "distancing devices" and "alienation effects" used by playwrights such as Thornton Wilder and Bertolt Brecht. In literary criticism, a similar device is known as "detachment." I will discuss these devices and techniques later in this chapter.

16. For a discussion and critique of Bullough's "antinomy of Distance," see Dickie et al., *Aesthetics*, pp. 48-60.

17. Long, "A 'Distanced' Art," p. 570.

To provide examples of how a performance can be underdistanced or overdistanced, Bullough returns to the theater. His first comedic example is when a "yokel" in the audience becomes so involved with the dangerous peril of a play's heroine that he leaps onto the stage to assist her. Distance is restored when the audience publicly reminds him that it's only a play. Bullough's second example is more psychological. Here he presents an "underdistanced" response from a man who arrives for the performance of *Othello* already suspicious and jealous concerning his wife. By a sudden reversal of perspective, he no longer sees a play or even a character named Othello, who apparently is betrayed by Desdemona; instead, he sees himself and his wife, and he thereby loses the necessary Distance (p. 99).

The same performance of Othello can provide an example of over-distancing: the thought processes of a drama expert and theater critic who are consumed by their "practical" activities. The result is a lack of emotional engagement. The same holds true of the audience member who, due to lack of experience with the theater or having no choice in attending the performance, concentrates on elaborate costumes and changing scenery. Such a perceptor is more impressed by the mechanics of the play and thus fails to comprehend or become involved in the actions of Othello, Desdemona, and Iago. These audience members could be described as lacking in imagination, involvement, and engagement by focusing on the "practical" aspects of the total work.[18] Because they were overdistanced, viewers who might have engaged with the drama were instead denied an aesthetic response. Both underdistancing and overdistancing can cause a loss of Distance and a loss of the possibility of an aesthetic experience. For Bullough, failure to distance is synonymous with failure to participate and appreciate.

---

18. Long, "A 'Distanced' Art," pp. 570, 571. For an extensive discussion of underdistancing and overdistancing, see Sheila Dawson, " 'Distancing' as an Aesthetic Principle," *Australasian Journal of Philosophy* 39, no. 2 (August 1961). A strong follower of Bullough, Dawson revised and reinterpreted his aesthetic of Distance for the mid-twentieth century. In further support of Bullough's understanding of Distance, see Sueh Pandit, "In Defense of Psychical Distance," *The British Journal of Aesthetics* 16 (1976): 56-60; see also Melvin Rader, "The Meaning of Art," in *A Modern Book of Esthetics* (New York: Holt, Rinehart, and Winston, 1979), pp. 14-17.

Distancing Techniques

Bullough identifies four components of art: the artist, the setting, the art object and its presentation, and the "perceptor," each having distinct distancing capabilities and characteristics. Using Bullough's example of the theater, we can see how Distance could be achieved through the distancing capabilities of these components: the actor, the theater, the play, and the audience.

For Bullough, the primary responsibility of the creative process begins with the artist, in this case the *actor*, whose "artistic production is the indirect formulation of a distanced mental context" (p. 115). The actor uses several factors to achieve Distance, such as costume and makeup, a trained voice, and stylized gestures. Distancing qualities of the *setting* would include "setting apart" the drama by lifting it up with a raised platform, framing it with a proscenium, and artificial lighting. Temporal distance may be achieved by the use of properties and scenery from a remote period.

Most important to Bullough's achievement of Distance is the art object's "formal" qualities. In the theater this would include symmetry, opposition, proportion, balance, and rhythm in the overall composition of the drama and its presentation through staging and direction.[19] Usually symmetry, proportion, and balance onstage are not considered distancing factors, but rather a part of composition whereby the work is made intelligible and enjoyable. In contrast, Bullough says: "For, every kind of visibly intentional arrangement of unification must, by the mere fact of its presence, enforce Distance, by distinguishing the object from the confused, disjointed and scattered forms of actual experience" (pp. 105-6). Because Distance comes between our own affections and the work of art, it takes qualities such as symmetry and balance and removes them from the disorganized chaos of the everyday world.

For the *audience member* at the play, the ability to achieve Distance would come via preparation and frequent encounters with theater. Bullough insists that a perceptor could cultivate Distance. For the underdistanced husband who sees *Othello* as an extension of his marital problems, awareness of the plot or the mechanics of the play itself could help

19. Long, "A 'Distanced' Art," p. 570.

him put this role aside. The overdistanced theater critic might benefit from an intentional to-and-fro movement — from emotional engagement to the critical distanced attitude.

The more the object becomes stylized, unrealistic, and isolated either by its own properties or through presentation, Distance correspondingly increases. As the perceptor adopts a less personal or emotionally involved posture with respect to the object or its presentation, Distance proportionally increases. Because of the "variability" of its components, Distance is not a fixed point but a continuum with "naturally changing degrees," depending on the art object, the recipient, and the presentation. Even so, Bullough makes clear his preference for the greatest aesthetic experience with the most intense and meaningful results: "What is, therefore, both in appreciation and production, most desirable is the *utmost decrease of Distance without its disappearance*" (p. 100; italics added).

Critics of Psychic Distance

As the discipline of aesthetics was being redefined in the mid-twentieth century, aesthetic attitude theory was challenged, and thus Distance as an aesthetic principle was scrutinized. Criticism of Bullough's low-distance aesthetic came from both sides of the spectrum. José Ortega y Gasset rejected low-distance art as being "human, all too human," in favor of stylistic, highly distanced art that serves as an "early warning system to society and culture."[20] At the same time, Bullough's aesthetic was also challenged by a strong countermovement to dehumanization, the goal of which was to break down Distance altogether. Bullough promoted a low-Distance art that was most desirable for "both appreciation and production"; yet he was against its disappearance altogether. He criticized such underdistanced work for referring to the body, sexuality, relevant and sensational topics of the day, and for expressing doubt as to the validity of

20. José Ortega y Gasset, "The Dehumanization of Art" (1925), from José Ortega y Gasset, *The Dehumanization of Art* (Princeton, NJ: Princeton University Press, 1948), quoted in Rader, *A Modern Book of Aesthetics*, pp. 333, 363-70; see also review by David Mandel, *Leonardo: International Journal of the Contemporary Artist* 8 (Winter 1975): 78, cited in Rader, *A Modern Book of Esthetics*, p. 333.

social institutions. What Bullough condemned in the countermovement, experimental theater embraced. It emphasized *engagement,* the intent to "break down the distance between artist and public, actor and audience, the work of art and the beholder."[21] Ironically, while this movement adamantly rejected Bullough's concept of Distance, its art was dependent on the function of Distance as a force to be continually broken down and destroyed in performance.

George Dickie, one of Bullough's strongest critics, claims that "aesthetic attitude theories" have run their course and no longer have theoretical value for aesthetics. In "All Aesthetic Attitude Theories Fail," he quotes Gilbert Ryle to that effect: "Myths often do a lot of theoretical good while they are new," but aesthetic attitude in general and psychic distance in particular are "no longer useful and in fact mislead aesthetic theory."[22] Dickie refers to Bullough's examples from the theater in which audience members were either underdistanced or overdistanced from the work of art. Using his own experience as an audience member, Dickie chides Bullough for confusing Distance with "intentions," thereby attempting a general theory of aesthetics based on an inattentive audience member. Dickie sums up what he calls Bullough's fallacy: "[S]ubstantive guidelines for art criticism and appreciation can be derived from the nature of a certain kind of psychological state. If there is no such psychological state, this approach is in serious difficulty."[23] More recently, Noël Carroll has also refuted Distance as an "experience aesthetic," affect-oriented and relying on the concept of disinterested attention. Drawing the same conclusions as does Dickie, she observes: "But upon scrutiny, this concept appears inadmissible, since it confuses motivation with attention. This suggests that the affect-oriented account of aesthetic experience is a dead end."[24]

While Bullough's foremost attempt was to provide an overall aesthetic based on Distance, he is better known today for his introduction of *dis-*

21. Rader, *A Modern Book of Aesthetics,* pp. 333-34.

22. George Dickie, "All Aesthetic Attitude Theories Fail: The Myth of the Aesthetic Attitude," in Dickie et al., *Aesthetics,* p. 342; Dickie, *Introduction to Aesthetics: An Analytic Approach* (New York: Oxford University Press, 1997).

23. Dickie, *Introduction to Aesthetics,* pp. 51-52.

24. Carroll, *Philosophy of Art,* p. 202.

tancing characteristics, or dynamics, in the four components of a work of art: the artist, the art object and its presentation, the spatial and temporal setting, and the perceptor or audience. The influence of what would later be called "distancing devices" in contemporary speech and performance cannot be overstated. Even Bullough's harshest critics, such as George Dickie, agree that Bullough's *dynamics of Distance*, especially with regard to the four components of a work of art, continue to be a significant influence in the performing arts and literature. M. H. Abrams observes that, in recent criticism, "the term *aesthetic distance*, or simply *distance*, is often used not only to define the nature of literary and aesthetic experience in general, but also to analyze the many devices by which authors control the degree of a reader's distance, or 'detachment' — which is in inverse relationship to the degree of a reader's involvement, or 'concern' — with the actions and fortunes of one or another character represented within a work of literature."[25] The dynamics of the relationship between distance and involvement for the reader/hearer/audience has been Bullough's legacy to contemporary speech performance and preaching.

Performing Distance

It is no coincidence that contemporary homileticians who discuss distance in preaching, notably Jana Childers and Charles Bartow, share a speech and performance-studies background. In the remainder of this chapter, I will investigate distance in speech performance by tracing its use in the disciplines of elocution, oral interpretation, presentational theater, and literary criticism that focuses on the reader as performer. With an eye toward preaching, I develop the following proposal: Distance between audience, performer, and text is integral to the *engagement of the hearer* in the performance as an event.[26]

25. Abrams, *A Glossary of Literary Terms*, p. 68.
26. For working definitions of the terms "oral interpretation," "interpretation," and "performance studies," see chapter 1 above. The term "interpretation" may include the practice and theory of oral reading and oral interpretation. For clarity, I will distinguish "interpretation" with regard to the performance of texts from hermeneutical theories of interpretation by the use of the term "oral interpretation."

Distance and Delivery: Elocution

> *Troilus* . . .
>   My will enkindled by mine eyes and ears,
>   Two traded pilots 'twixt the dangerous shores
>   Of will and judgment. . . .
>
> William Shakespeare,
Troilus and Cressida, II.ii.61-65[27]

In "The Dangerous Shores: From Elocution to Interpretation," Wallace Bacon uses Shakespeare's image of "dangerous shores" as a metaphor for a polarity in performance where "delivery" is on one shore and "text" is on the other (pp. 148-52). While Troilus's dichotomy was between judgment and the will as "enkindled" by the senses of sight and sound, Bacon observes a similar dichotomy in theories of performance where the double character of the subject (text and delivery) can be stated in a series of compounds: reason-passion, logic-emotion, scholarship-entertainment, content-delivery, natural-mechanical, and — especially germane to this project — *text-audience.* Bacon declares: "Too much interest in the audience is as bad as too exclusive interest in text — another way of looking at the dangerous shores" (p. 151).

For Bacon, all these bifurcations simply underscore the dilemma that "exists, has always existed, and always will exist" in the performance of texts: "The whole art consists, has always consisted, and always will consist in a union of the two elements. It has not in the long run worked to overlook the basic and determining character of the text being read; neither will it work to overlook the essential significance of the oral performance" (p. 150). According to Bacon, the history of the performance of texts has always involved the interplay between text and delivery; yet different schools of thought at different times have emphasized one over the other. Continuing Bacon's metaphor, the emphasis of the elocutionary movement lands it on the "shore" of delivery.

---

27. Quoted in Wallace A. Bacon, "The Dangerous Shores: From Elocution to Interpretation," *Quarterly Journal of Speech* 46, no. 2 (April 1960): 149. Hereafter, page references to this journal article appear in parentheses in the text.

Elocution is best known as a speech movement and part of a liberal education in eighteenth- and nineteenth-century England and America. Although elocution is often associated with public speeches and performances of literature for inspiration and entertainment, its roots are liturgical, going back to the delivery of sermons in the seventeenth century.[28] "Elocution" is derived from classical rhetoric's term *elocutio*, usually interpreted as the style of the speaker's composition. The change in meaning of *elocutio* from the "style" of the composition to "delivery" is often attributed to John Mason's "Essay on Elocution," published in 1748. However, a hundred years earlier, clergyman John Wilkins had used the term for the delivery of sermons. In his essay *Ecclesiastes, or, A Discourse concerning the Gift of Preaching*, published in 1646, Wilkins uses the term to note a shift from the sermon's style, according to classical rhetoric, to the preacher's *actio*, or "delivery," best suited to the office of preacher. He says, "The most proper manner of eloquution is with modesty and gravity, which will best sute with our calling and businesse."[29]

In his eight famous lectures delivered in London in 1762, Thomas Sheridan, actor, elocutionist, and son of an Anglican theologian and preacher, defined "elocution" as "the just and graceful management of the voice, countenance, and gesture in speaking."[30] His lectures were mainly concerned with pronunciation, accent, emphasis, tones, pauses, pitch, and gesture. Particularly related to the emotions were tones and gesture. According to Sheridan, tones were the audible aspects of emotion, and gestures were the visible aspects of emotion. Each passion had its own corresponding tone and peculiar look or gesture with the body. All the other elements of delivery were related particularly to the expression of ideas (Bacon, p. 148).

Throughout the eighteenth and greater part of the nineteenth centuries, "elocution" referred to effective speaking and the delivery of spoken forms of discourse. It became "the art of expressive thought by speech"

28. Giles Wilkeson Gray, "What Was Elocution?" *The Quarterly Journal of Speech* 46, no. 1 (1960): 2.

29. Wilbur Samuel Howell, "Sources of the Elocutionary Movement in England, 1700-1748," *The Quarterly Journal of Speech* 45 (1959): 5, cited by Gray, "What Was Elocution?" p. 2.

30. Thomas Sheridan (1719-1788), "A Course of Lectures on Elocution" (London, 1762), cited in Bacon, "Dangerous Shores," p. 148.

and was later defined as the "Art of expressing thought and feeling by means of Voice and Action."[31] Though elocution emphasized the elements of delivery according to their corresponding emotions and ideas, it was not at the expense of meaning in the act of speaking. Bacon observes: "The eighteenth-century term elocution embraced not alone the classical concept of 'style of composition,' but the whole conveyance of meaning through style of composition *delivered*" (p. 149).[32] By today's standards, corresponding elements of delivery with particular emotions and thought and their subsequent codification may seem mechanical and contrived. Charles L. Bartow notes that, whereas today the term "elocution" might evoke "guffaws," in the mid-eighteenth century, elocution, at its best, referred to "the management of voice and body in the speaking of texts and in the presentation of formal addresses."[33] Whereas today's dictionary may define the term in a derogatory sense as a "stilted, artificial manner of delivery," Bartow reminds us that the Latin origin of the word simply means to "speak out," and in classical rhetoric, *elocutio* was "a speaker's distinctive way of bringing thought to expression."[34] The external elements of delivery were not an imposition but part of a conventional and normative view. Although the emphasis was on performance, this view recognized "sense" as the determining event from which all passions in delivery must arise and be fixed (Bacon, pp. 148-52).[35]

A number of influences combined to bring about the demise of elocution in the latter part of the nineteenth century. One factor was its being severed from the delivery of all forms of spoken discourse to being associated essentially with reading aloud or simply "performing." As a result,

---

31. Anna T. Randall, *Reading and Elocution: Theoretical and Practical* (New York: Ivison, Blakeman, Taylor, 1869), p. xiii; and William T. Ross, *Voice, Culture and Elocution* (New York: Baker and Taylor, 1887), p. 1, cited in Gray, "What Was Elocution?" p. 3. These definitions of elocution paved the way for the early twentieth-century designation of oral reading as "expression."

32. Bacon says that in the eighteenth and nineteenth centuries, teachers of the art of speech and reading did not normally distinguish between these arts but regarded them as nearly identical.

33. Charles L. Bartow, "In Service to the Servants of the Word: Teaching Speech at Princeton Seminary," *The Princeton Seminary Bulletin* 13, no. 3 (1992): 275.

34. Bartow, "In Service to the Servants of the Word," p. 275.

35. See also Gray, "What Was Elocution?" pp. 1-7.

elocution lost contact with the canons of rhetoric pertaining to speeches, sermons, and literature, and thus delivery became divorced from content. A second factor was elocution's abandonment of the theories and philosophies of its early writers for the mysticism of the time in America, especially influenced by the theories of Delsarte. When text and "sense" had been severed from delivery, it was replaced with a mystical absorption into nature or other forms of art, what Bullough described as crudely naturalistic, harrowing, and repulsive, without distance between the work and the performer. Since there was no longer a text to be delivered, "expression" became "possession," producing performances that had degenerated into bird calls, imitations of children, or statue-posing.[36]

A third factor for the movement's falling from grace was that elocution had become an idiosyncratic "art unto itself." Materials were being written and performed for no purpose other than displaying the oratorical versatility of the speaker. Symbolic of this shift to the performer was the tacking on of the suffix "ist" to "elocution": no longer designated as "readers" or "speakers" (terms that imply a text, speech, or even sermon), performers were now called "elocutionists," practitioners of the art of delivery with nothing to deliver.[37] Performers performed themselves. Preachers preached their delivery.

Although the emphasis in elocution had been on "expression," there was *something* to be expressed. When elocution became separated from text, what remained were the mechanics and spectacle of the elocutionist and the effect on the audience (or congregation). Returning to Wallace Bacon's opening metaphor of the two shores, the *distance* between the text and performer had collapsed. Without a *text*, elocution crashed into the dangerous shore of *delivery*, and there met its demise.

Distance and Text: Oral Interpretation

In the twentieth century, elocution was followed by the modern discipline of "oral interpretation," later called "interpretation." Both disci-

---

36. Randall, *Reading and Elocution*, pp. 1-7; Bullough, *Aesthetics*, p. 101.
37. Randall, *Reading and Elocution*, p. 7.

plines involved the performance of texts, yet each with a different emphasis. Thomas Sheridan defined elocution as "the just and graceful management of the voice, countenance, and gesture in speaking" (Bacon, p. 149); by contrast, Wallace Bacon defined "interpretation" in 1959 as "the study of literature through the medium of oral performance" (pp. v-ix, 149).[38] Bacon notes that it is important to underscore that both definitions reveal interest in the fundamental contributions of the oral performance and in neither is literary appreciation viewed apart from delivery. But when the two are compared, Sheridan's definition of elocution uses the text as a point of departure, whereas Bacon's definition of interpretation uses the text as a point of return. According to Bacon, this seems to be the clear line of change from the eighteenth century to the mid-twentieth century regarding the teaching and practice of oral reading (p. 149).

In contrast to the later elocutionists, who emphasized technique and its effect on the audience, interpretation in the 1950s was moving in the direction of the "thing read," not in the direction of the "person reading." This is not to say that participation on the part of the performer (or audience) was not important. What was important was the participation *in the life of the text.* For the oral interpreter, understanding is necessary for participation; yet participation through performance creates a new understanding of the text. Whether this understanding is deliberate or intuitive, it involves knowledge (p. 150).

In "The Dangerous Shores," Bacon lists three things involved in the interpretation process: the text ("the interpreter's excuse for being"), audibility, and aliveness (pp. 148-52).[39] The latter two involve the performer and the audience. In *The Art of Interpretation,* Bacon contrasts the oral interpreter to the silent reader, observing that the unique function of the interpreter is to create a "presence" and to create it so fully that it can contain and involve an audience.[40] *Presence* is not the text acting on the interpreter

38. See also Wallace A. Bacon and Robert S. Breen, preface to *Literature as Experience* (New York: McGraw-Hill, 1959).

39. Discussed in Alla Bozarth-Campbell, *The Word's Body: An Incarnational Aesthetic of Interpretation* (Tuscaloosa: University of Alabama Press, 1979), pp. 18-19.

40. Wallace A. Bacon, *The Art of Interpretation* (New York: Holt, Rinehart and Winston, 1979), p. xii, cited in Bozarth-Campbell, *The Word's Body,* p. 18.

alone or the interpreter acting on the text alone, but the dialogic yielding of their interaction. In response to Bacon's "shores" of text on the one hand and delivery on the other, Alla Bozarth-Campbell observes that the art of interpretation is always "balanced, dynamically poised between these two constituents." Describing Bacon's understanding of interpretation, Bozarth-Campbell says:

> Balance consists in the union of logic and emotion, reason and passion, and so on, which is to be determined, not by the idiosyncratic performer, but solely by the "determining character of the text." This union implies participation in the life of the text — participation that follows from understanding. The art of interpretation, according to this position, is "an art of enactment, of embodiment, of becoming. The poem is active, the reader active; the art of interpretation aims at establishing in oral performance a congruence between these two sets of acts."[41]

In interpretation, the oral performance of texts, the interpreter's goal is to achieve a "balance" between text and performer, and between performer and audience. The dynamic necessary to preserve this balance is identified as distance.

Distance and Modes

Distance has long been a subject of discussion and research in interpretation theory and pedagogy. Wallace Bacon and Leland H. Roloff have identified the dynamics of distance within the text according to the "modes" of literature. Modes refer to classifications of literature based on the voice of the author in the text. In *The Art of Interpretation*, Bacon suggests that the identification of "modes" attempts to get at matters of perspective, locus, and presence. Based on Aristotle's classification of the *lyric, dramatic*, and *epic, lyric* is the mode in which the author speaks, or seems to speak, in his or her own voice and stands in the closest and most immediate rela-

---

41. Bacon, "Dangerous Shores," p. 150; see also Bacon, *The Art of Interpretation*, p. xii, cited in Bozarth-Campbell, *The Word's Body*, p. 19.

tionship to the audience. *Epic* is the mode in which the speaker functions as a narrator, sometimes speaking in his or her own voice directly to the audience and at other times through the voice of others — in which the characters seem to speak for themselves.[42] *Dramatic* is the mode in which the voice of the author — or what we may take to be the author's voice — is entirely submerged into the voice of characters. For Bacon and Roloff, modality cuts across all literary genres and is based on the distant/near and direct/indirect relationship between the author and text as faithfully presented by the performer to the audience.[43]

All three modes can be seen in Scripture. A Pauline epistle is lyric, with direct address that provides a close relationship between the author and the hearer, whereas the Gospel of Mark is epic: the author sometimes speaks directly to the audience and at other times through the voice of characters. In the Bible, as in other texts that are a product of redaction and compilation, the dramatic mode may take on a different modality depending on the author and the context. For example, the song of Miriam may have been lyric, but it becomes epic when put in the context of the book Exodus's story.

Distinctions between modes become even less clear when texts are performed. No longer can a particular mode be identified according to the "nearness" or "distance" of an author or implied author. In performance, nearness and distance do not necessarily correspond to lyric/epic/dramatic. The performed voice in the lyric mode may be distant and introspective, giving the audience a look into the speaker's inner thoughts; or the performer might directly address the audience members and draw them *near* with the intensity of eye contact and "open focus." The same holds true of the dramatic mode, depending on whether or not the character is believable and compelling.

Even so, Roloff affirms that the relationship between the author's voice and the text is what governs distance in performance. In *The Perception and Evocation of Literature*, he proposes that performance is guided by three main considerations:

42. Here the term "epic" is not to be confused with the literary genre of saga.

43. Bacon, *The Art of Interpretation*, pp. 244-46; Leland H. Roloff, *The Perception and Evocation of Literature* (Glenview, IL: Scott, Foresman, 1973), pp. 64-66.

1. The aesthetic distance in performance is determined by the literature and not by the performer.
2. The performer is the source of the aesthetic enjoyment, not the literature. Here he refutes the theory that literature is some kind of abstract "object" that exists between the performer and audience.
3. The audience may, and usually does, hold the performer accountable for the interpretation as well as the mastery and control of the literary work.

The performer determines appropriate distance by attending to the modality of the text through the use of intuition. According to Roloff, the sensitive reader or performer "apprehends or intuits the distance the work requires."[44] From these criteria, it is evident that the literature itself determines the distance between the performer and text.

In recent years, *The Art of Interpretation*'s criteria for distance in performance have been challenged as being based on an outmoded understanding of aesthetic distance. Following the rethinking of Bullough's work in aesthetics, the wealth of material that was published in the 1940s on the principle of aesthetic distance in oral interpretation began to emphasize the process of distancing or distancing devices in the 1960s and 1970s. Beverly Whitaker Long presents a compelling argument that in mid-century the predominant theory of aesthetic distance was based on a hermeneutic that perceived the text as being autonomous from the performer and the performance. Distance was required of the performer so that she or he would not absorb or violate the text and the "intentions" of the author. These intentions should be recognized according to the conventions used in the text. When placed on a continuum, distance increases when moving from left to right:

conversation	- - - - -	rhythmical utterance
prose	- - - - - - - -	verse
colloquial speech	- - - -	elevated diction
direct address	- - - - -	dialogue between characters
topical subjects	- - - - -	imaginative subjects

44. Roloff, *Perception and Evocation*, pp. 100, 104.

The correct form of distance between performer and audience depended on the location of the conventions of speech on the above continuum. Various diagrams were created by which a genre of performance could be "scientifically" located and defined according to "aesthetic distance." Drama, for example, required less distance from the actor to the play and more distance to the audience, whereas oral interpretation or the "reading aloud" of a piece required greater distance between reader and text and less between text and audience. When the use of distance did not match these conventions, the "intention" of the text was considered violated and the performance was deemed unsuccessful.[45]

In the 1970s, a scientific approach to distance in performance disappeared when its underlying principles gave way to a "New Hermeneutic." No longer could "distance" define strict genres. Charts plotting criteria for aesthetic distance disappeared when the New Hermeneutic claimed that the meaning of texts in performance was inseparable from the "pretexts" and "contexts" of performer *and* audience.

Distance and the Audience: Presentational Theater

Presentational performance can best be understood in contrast to its more modern counterpart, representational performance.[46] *Representational performance,* or "representationalism," is the theory and practice of drama that portrays or "represents" the real world and emphasizes the illusion of reality. In contemporary proscenium theater, it is staged as if a fourth wall has been removed and the audience is privy to the slice of life behind that wall. The characters appear as if they are not aware that they are being observed. Costumes, sets, staging, and technical aspects of the

---

45. Long, "A 'Distanced' Art," pp. 572-83.

46. Unless otherwise noted, references to representational and presentational performance are a compilation based on the following: Charlotte Lee and Frank Galati, *Oral Interpretation* (Boston: Houghton Mifflin, 1977), pp. 383-89; Bacon, *The Art of Interpretation* pp. 244-46, 458, 500-503, 532; Jack A. Vaughn, *Drama A to Z* (New York: Frederick Ungar, 1978), pp. 6, 57, 72, 138, 150, 214-15, and lectures at The School of Speech, Northwestern University, 1982-84.

performance are not symbolic but accurate — or "realistic" to the setting and time period of the drama.

In representational performance, actors do not present a character; they portray a role. They become the characters that they portray. Constantine Stanislavski (1865-1938), a master teacher of representational performance, taught actors to live their part outside of the performance in order to train the entire body. The aim was to reproduce accurately realistic emotional affect in performance. He says: "The actor lives his part only as a preparation for perfecting an external form. . . . Once that is determined he reproduces that form through the aid of mechanically trained muscles. . . . Living your role is not the chief moment of creation . . . but one of the preparatory stages for further artistic work."

In representational drama, the imitation of form is as important as the content or the message of the play, for anything the audience perceives as less than accurate breaks the illusion of the created reality. For Stanislavski, "[t]he art of representation demands perfection if it is to remain an art."[47] Anything less distances the audience through distraction.

For representational performance to be successful, the audience must participate in a "willing suspension of disbelief." The English poet Samuel Taylor Coleridge (1772-1834) popularized that phrase — concerning the basis on which "poetic faith" operates in literature. In accordance with modern aesthetic theory, we approach literature with a sense of disbelief, knowing that the character and actions portrayed are not immediately real to us. Yet, because we want to participate in another reality — the world of the text or artistic creation — we voluntarily choose to suspend for the moment our disbelief and accept as "real" the artistic representation.[48] When applied to theater and performance, Coleridge's "willing suspension of disbelief" is an explanation of our faith in the truth of a representation on a stage. The audience approaches the performance with an *optique du théâtre* (a "theater lens"), or, less literally, a "stage illusion" that serves as a reminder that at all times the play is fiction and not reality.[49] In order

47. Constantine Stanislavski, *An Actor's Handbook*, trans. and ed. Elizabeth Reynolds Hapgood (New York: Theatre Arts Books, 1963), pp. 119-20.

48. Samuel Taylor Coleridge, *Biographia Literaria* (1817), chap. 14, quoted in Vaughn, *Drama A to Z*, pp. 214-15.

49. This term was made popular by English drama critic George Henry Lewes

for the representational performance to be more than artifice — unreal and therefore "false" — the audience members suspend their disbelief and participate in the new reality being offered. The greater the actor's and technician's skill in creating the illusion of "real life," the smaller the need for the audience's "willing suspension of disbelief" in order for the performance event to be successful.

Representational theater was taken to the extreme at the turn of the twentieth century in France with the Théâtre Libre in Paris and in the United States with producers such as David Belasco.[50] Although both of these dramatic schools strove for absolute realism, to the point of real props and actors turning their backs to the audience, they could not overcome the predisposition of the audience entering the theater to know and expect that the world represented onstage was still a fiction. By virtue of its being a performance, representational drama is still always partly presentational.

In contrast to representational performance, the aim of presentational performance is not to imitate "real life" and therefore create an illusion, but to present for the audience a creative fictive world. In presentational performance, *how* the drama is portrayed is as important to meaning and experience as the *who* or *what* of the play. Therefore, dramatic devices and artifice are not hidden for illusion's sake but intentionally highlighted in performance for the sake of wonder, aesthetic pleasure, meaning, and reflection.

In Western civilization, presentational performance has a long history that can be seen in the theatrical styles of Europe and traced back to the ancient Greek theater. For the Greeks, the role of the actor was symbolic, standing for and "suggesting" the actions of the gods and great mortals. Often the highlight of a festival in honor of a god, the ritual of the presentation focused on the audience's belief not in the present and immediate illusion of reality but in the reenactment, interpretation, and thus meaning of the story. Especially when the story was well known, the Greeks were as much interested in the reenactment — and hence the aesthetic quality of the performance — as in the particular interpretation of one playwright in

---

(1817-1878), borrowing from French actor François René Molé. See Vaughn, *Drama A to Z*, pp. 138-39.

50. Vaughn, *Drama A to Z*, p. 162.

contrast to another. According to scholars, Greek audiences were curious about how stories of well-known characters such as Orestes and Electra would be handled by Euripides compared to how Aeschylus would handle them. An emphasis on different interpretations fostered critical reflection by the audience on various meanings of the story with regard to religion, morality, and politics.

Greek theater used many nonrealistic dramatic devices that later flourished on the Elizabethan stage and can be presently seen in contemporary theater and performance. These presentational forms involve the stage, chorus, songs, narrator, and masks. In the Greek theater there was no imaginary fourth wall of the proscenium stage, but an amphitheater with a stage in the half- or three-quarter-round arrangement similar to the Elizabethan stage or the contemporary thrust stage. Compared to the contemporary proscenium theater, where the raising of the curtain invites us to observe through a fourth wall and enter inside the drama, the Greek stage and its contemporary offshoots thrust or project the world of the performance out into the audience, where they would participate and complete "suggested actions" in their own imaginations. The chorus played an important part in Greek theater, for it not only physically occupied the projected space of the stage but also projected its reflection onto the action and characters. The chorus provided commentary — sometimes *to* the audience and at other times speaking *for* the audience regarding the drama. Masks served not only to assist in vocal amplification and projection, but also amplified and projected in a "frozen gaze" the inner emotional state of a character that may have been externally restrained or concealed by a person in real life.[51]

In presentational performance, all of these dramatic devices serve as distancing techniques between the performance and audience. Whereas representational theater encourages closeness and empathy with the characters and their situation, presentational performance encourages contemplation of the characters and dramatic action and their significance through *distancing* the audience. When drama is represented, the audience observes and participates in the story; when drama is presented, the story becomes a *part of* the audience.

51. Lee and Galati, *Oral Interpretation*, p. 384.

Distancing Techniques

Two of the most influential modern dramatists to make use of presentation conventions of distancing were Thornton Wilder (1879-1975) and Bertolt Brecht (1898-1956). In the plays of Thornton Wilder, the technique of distancing in the theater was to evoke wonder — wonder at the "enchantment of the theater's power of illusion and wonder at the human condition as revealed in the theater." Distancing also evoked a contemplation of values. Wilder observes in the preface to a collection of his plays: "*Our Town* is not offered as a picture of life in a New Hampshire village; or as a speculation about conditions of life after death. . . . It is an attempt to find a value above all price for the smallest events in our daily life."[52]

Wilder promotes this contemplation of values and wonder of the human condition by distancing the audience from a particular setting in which the plot, characters, and action take place. Compared to the realistic settings, or "scenery," of traditional representational theater, the set for *Our Town* is made up of a few chairs, tables, and ladders that diminish as the play proceeds. A ladder becomes a wall, a tree, a stairway in a house, and even a metaphor for a vista of the heavens. By distancing the audience from a particular setting, says Wilder, "I have made a claim as preposterous as possible, for I have set the village against the larger dimension of time and place" (p. xi). Through this intentional separation of the play from the setting, along with the direct address of a "stage manager" narrator and the unconversational (or "unreal") repetition of words such as "hundreds," "thousands," and "millions," the play is presented to the audience and completed within the audience's imagination. Wilder suggests: "Our claim, our hope, our despair are in the mind — not in things, not in 'scenery' . . . . [T]he climax of this play needs only five square feet of boarding and the passion to know what life means to us" (p. xii).

Intentional distance through setting is a technique also found in Wilder's play *The Skin of Our Teeth*. Beginning with the opening scene, the audience is forced to "back up" from the action of the play in order to make

52. Thornton Wilder, preface to *Three Plays by Thornton Wilder: Our Town, The Skin of Our Teeth, The Matchmaker* (New York: Bantam Books, 1961), p. xi. Hereafter, page references to this work appear in parentheses in the text.

35

sense of the shifts in time and space. They soon recognize that they are observing a family living in two times at once: in prehistoric time and in a contemporary New Jersey commuter suburb. The audience is forced beyond empathy with particular characters to contemplation of the human condition — whence we came and whither we are going. Through the use of distancing devices, Wilder removes the usual theatrical distractions and raises to the attention of the audience the essential meaning of the drama. He clearly declares: "I am not an innovator but a rediscoverer of forgotten goods and I hope a remover of obtrusive bric-a-brac" (p. xi).

Alienation Devices

A dramatist who rediscovered presentational theater and took it in a new direction is Bertolt Brecht. Brecht's "epic theater" has profoundly influenced twentieth-century theater, both in theory and practice.[53] A noted feature of Brecht's epic theater was his use of *Verfremdungseffekt* (alienation, or "alienation devices"). Brecht was opposed to the traditional representational theater of his time, which promoted an illusion of reality. According to Brecht, the traditional play casts a "spell" over the audience, a spell in which the audience members are either mesmerized into a state in which time, space, and self-awareness are suspended, or they are empathetically absorbed into the emotions of the characters and the pathos of the play. In either case, critical consciousness is lost. The audience would leave the theater entertained, moved, or individually pondering, but the audience as a whole was not transformed or moved toward action. Brecht criticized traditional theater's supporting of the status and values of the middle and upper class through entertainment, emotional catharsis, and private transformation, while ignoring the public, social, and political power of performance.[54]

53. Epic theater was first developed by the German director Erwin Piscator in the late 1920s, but it has mainly become associated with the plays and techniques of Brecht, who spent time directing his work in the United States, where he significantly influenced American drama.

54. See Vaughn, *Drama A to Z*, pp. 8, 72; Richard Schechner, *Performance Theory* (New York: Routledge, 1988), pp. 120-59; Beverly Whitaker Long and Mary Francis Hop-

Vehemently opposed to this privatized experience of drama, Brecht used techniques that were boldly theatrical, whereby the audience was "alienated" or estranged from the illusion or emotions on stage. Whereas Thornton Wilder's aim of presentational was "wonder" and the "pondering of the meaning of the human condition," Brecht's use of alienation devices created critical distance to evoke a critique of society and a transformation of the audience into a community of social action. To this social and political end, epic theater used songs, narration, episodic (nonsequential plotting of) scenes, and openly displayed theater devices and technology. A half curtain or no curtain at all, exposed lighting, and open changes of scenery served as a constant reminder that the audience members were not to get lost in the plot or the characters, that they were attending a production in order to think, learn and act.

Compared to Stanislavski's method, in which actors were to display realistic emotion in a realistic way, Brecht's actors broke the illusion by putting on and taking off roles and characters in front of the audience, much in the same way the ancient Greek actor would put on or take off a mask. One of the ways this device was used was to call the audience's attention to the fact that in public life we all play different roles, and that those in political, religious, and economic power are to be suspected of playing theatrical deceptions. Characters were not to evoke empathy but critical distance.

Perhaps Brecht's most powerful alienation device was the jarring use of visual aids. In the middle of an engaging scene or a moving dramatic monologue, the moment would be invaded by a film, slide, newspaper headline, or signboard that was dropped onto the stage and gave social commentary on the speech and actions of the play. *Saint Joan of the Stockyards* (also translated as *Saint Joan of the Slaughterhouse*) is set in the Chicago stockyards during the middle of a labor dispute involving management ("meat king"), meat packers, stockbreeders, brokers, the poor, the media, soldiers (the police), and officers of the "Black Straw Hats"

---

kins, *Performing Literature: An Introduction to Oral Interpretation* (Englewood Cliffs, NJ: Prentice Hall, 1982), pp. 151-53. For an in-depth discussion by Brecht on epic theater, see "Short Description of a New Technique of Acting Which Produces an Alienation Effect," in Michael Huxley and Noel Witts, eds., *The Twentieth Century Performance Reader* (New York: Routledge, 1996).

(Brecht's version of the Salvation Army). Joan, a lieutenant in the Black Straw Hats, is a voice for justice for the workers and in solidarity with the poor. It would be easy for audience members to become absorbed into the plot of the story and empathetically lost in Joan's passion for justice; but Brecht does not expect the suspense of the conflict or the passion of Joan's speeches to move the audience toward political action. For Brecht, such emotional catharsis is usually accompanied by social complacency when the play has ended.

To keep the audience from getting too close to this story, he has pertinent news headlines from around the world announced over loudspeakers behind the audience during the dialogue, a reminder that the drama has economic and political implications on a global scale. Throughout the play, placards are obtrusively placed in front of each scene to summarize what is to follow. For example:

TO ASSUAGE THE MISERY OF THE STOCKYARDS, THE BLACK STRAW HATS SALLY FORTH FROM THEIR MISSION HOUSE: JOAN'S FIRST DESCENT INTO THE DEPTHS.[55]

The manner of a heading in a silent-screen melodrama and in the terse style of a newscaster has the effect of removing the suspense of plot, and the audience is distanced from involvement in the immediate action.

Brecht's "alienation devices" diminished the accumulation of suspense and discouraged traditional spectator involvement, thereby promoting critical reflection on the social and political implications of the play. By distancing the audience from the world of the play onstage, he challenged the audience to draw the play *near to the outside world.*

Between Ritual and Theater

Alienation devices do not mean audience disengagement or lack of interest. The play is not reduced to a flat moral fable or a dull informative

---

55. Bertolt Brecht, *Collected Plays*, vol. 3, part 1, trans. Ralph Manheim, ed. John Willett and Ralph Manheim (London: Methuen, 1991), p. 7.

illustration for political propaganda. Richard Schechner, in *Performance Theory*, says that distancing promotes engagement. Noting Brecht's and other dramatists' use of distancing techniques, Schechner observes that presentational performance may decrease the suspense of plot but may increase the "tensive" nature of the performance by moving back and forth between the two poles of "Efficacy/Ritual" and "Entertainment/Theatre." Whether a performance is called a "ritual" or "theater" depends mainly on context and function: where it is performed, by whom, and under what function. Schechner creates the following polarity:

EFFICACY ←	→ ENTERTAINMENT
Ritual	*Theatre*
results	fun
link to an absent Other	only for those here
symbolic time	emphasis now
performer possessed, in trance	performer knows what s/he's doing
audience participates	audience watches
audience believes	audience appreciates
criticism discouraged	criticism flourishes
collective creativity	individual creativity[56]

Although we might place Sunday morning worship under the categories of "efficacy" and "ritual," and a Broadway musical under the heading "entertainment and theater," Schechner makes it clear that in all performances various movements of the listed characteristics take place between the two poles at different times. For Wilder, presentational forms shifted theater back to ritual, where the emphasis on now was moved to "symbolic time," the audience's "appreciation" moved toward "belief," and, especially in *Our Town*, an experience of the "only for those here" hinted at a collective "link to an absent other." In Brecht's epic theater, the purpose of alienation devices was to redirect theater from being "fun" private entertainment to being "collective creativity," which brings forth "results" — such as community transformation.

---

56. Schechner, *Performance Theory*, pp. 120-59.

Distance and the Reader: Reading as Performance

As distance as an aesthetic principle began to wane in mid-twentieth-century philosophy, interpretation, and performance theory, its popularity increased as characteristics or devices in literary criticism. Especially in narrative criticism, distance was used to analyze the author's control of the detachment of the reader in contrast to involvement, empathy, or concern of the reader toward characters represented in a work of literature. The degree of distance between reader and character was usually determined first by the narrator.

A prime analysis of the function of distance in narrative is Wayne C. Booth's "Control of 'Distance' in Jane Austen's 'Emma,'" in his *The Rhetoric of Fiction*. Here Booth discusses how the reader's distance is achieved by the author toward the character Emma through sympathy and judgment, humor and comedy, the control of "inside views" of the character, dramatic irony, and the reader's trust that the narrator and the author are "reliable." The complexities and changing nature of the reader's distance toward the character is expressed in Jane Austen's description of Emma: "A heroine whom no one but myself will much like."[57]

Narrative critic Gerald Prince proposes "narratee" as a more precise term for the one being addressed by the narrator in a given narrative. He says that most critics confuse narratee with adjacent notions of receptor (*récepteur*), reader, and arch-reader (*archilecteur*). In "Introduction to the Study of the Narratee," he writes: "As there are often several narrators, several narratees, and several characters in the text, the complexity of the rapports and the variety of the *distances* that are established between them can be quite complex." Prince notes that a dialogue between narrators, narratees, and characters develops as a function of distance that separates them from each other. As the dialogue develops, so does the narration. Prince says that "these rapports and these distances determine to a great extent the way in which certain values are praised and others are rejected in the course of a narration and the way in which certain events are emphasized and others are nearly passed over in silence." Complexities in

57. Wayne C. Booth, *The Rhetoric of Fiction* (Chicago: University of Chicago Press, 1983), pp. 242-66.

plot or situation can result from the instability of the distances between narrator, narratee, and the characters; and the distance that separates the narratee from the ideal, virtual, or real readers can "determine the tone and the very nature of the narration."[58]

In the criticism of Booth and Prince, distance between narrators, characters, and the reader (or narratee) is determined by and contained within the text itself. In opposition, Louise Rosenblatt introduces the actual reader as being a part of the literary work. In *Literature as Exploration* (1938), and later in *The Reader, the Text, the Poem: The Transactional Theory of the Literary Work* (1978), Rosenblatt advances a transactional theory of literature where literary experience is reciprocal between the reader and the text. She observes: "My insistence on the term transaction is a means of establishing the active role of both reader and text in interpretation, and ensures that we recognize that any interpretation is an event occurring at a particular time in a particular social or cultural context. Once the work has been evoked, it can become the object of reflection and analysis, according to the various critical and scholarly approaches."[59]

In opposition to the New Criticism of her time, Rosenblatt argued that meaning is not found in the text alone: "A novel or poem or play remains merely inkspots on paper until a reader transforms them into a set of meaningful symbols. The literary work exists in the live circuit set up between reader and text: the reader infuses intellectual and emotional meanings into the pattern of verbal symbols, and those symbols channel his or her thoughts and feelings. Out of this complex process emerges a more or less organized imaginative experience."[60]

Whereas meaning is not located in the text, neither is it "absorbed" exclusively into the reader, as in some versions of *subjective* criticism and

58. Gerald Prince, "Introduction to the Study of the Narratee," in Jane P. Tompkins, ed., *Reader-Response Criticism: From Formalism to Post-Structuralism* (Baltimore: Johns Hopkins University Press, 1980), pp. 19-20 (italics added).

59. Louise M. Rosenblatt, "Reaffirming *Literature as Exploration*," in Edmund J. Farrell and James R. Squire, eds., *Transactions with Literature: A Fifty-Year Perspective* (Urbana, IL: National Council of Teachers of English, 1990), p. 106.

60. Louise M. Rosenblatt, *Literature as Exploration* (New York: Noble and Noble, 1976), p. 25.

reader-response criticism. These extreme reader-oriented movements, with which she has sometimes mistakenly been identified, arose after Rosenblatt's original work. She says: *"Under the guidance of the text,* out of his own thoughts, and feelings and sensibilities, the reader makes a new ordering, the formed substance which is for him the literary work of art."[61] For Rosenblatt, the reader's responses *and* the text are in transaction whereby the text is performed by the reader as an *event.* Meaning is found in that transactional event.[62]

The reader, whether silent or aloud, who adopts an aesthetic posture toward a text is a *performer:* "In the evocation of literary works of art, then, the reader calls forth the thoughts, images, situations, and characters from the printed words. The complexity of the aesthetic process rests on the extent to which 'meaning' resides in the felt experience, in the kinesthetic sensations, the associations, the affective coloring derived from past encounters with words and their referents in life and in literature."[63]

In transactional theory, distance is not limited to a narrative device, located within a text, that informs the empathy or detachment of the reader to characters or the narrator. Nor is it a dispassionate, detached, or aesthetic distance, such as was promoted by Kant, Bullough, and some of the New Critics. Rosenblatt cites her article "The Poem as Event" (1964) as the "first explicit attack on the New Critics that called for a criticism based on the reader's response."[64] Although sympathetic with the New Critics' concept of the intentional fallacy, in which the meaning of a text is freed from its authorial intent, she is directly opposed to their understanding of the affective fallacy, because it dismisses what a reader brings to a text and the responses evoked in the reader by the text.

In *Art and Engagement* (1991), Arnold Berleant, a philosopher of aes-

---

61. Louise M. Rosenblatt, *Literature as Exploration* (New York: D. Appleton-Century, 1968), quoted in Edward Quinn, *Literary and Thematic Terms* (New York: Checkmark Books, 2000), p. 330 (italics added).

62. Rosenblatt, *Literature as Exploration;* Louise M. Rosenblatt, *The Reader, the Text, the Poem: The Transactional Theory of the Literary Work* (Carbondale, IL: Southern Illinois University Press, 1978); Louise M. Rosenblatt, "Act 1, Scene 1: Enter the Reader," *Literature in Performance* 1, no. 2 (1981): 13-23; Rosenblatt, "Reaffirming *Literature as Exploration,*" pp. 97-107.

63. Rosenblatt, "Act 1, Scene 1: Enter the Reader," p. 18.

64. Rosenblatt, "Reaffirming *Literature as Exploration,*" p. 103.

thetics, provides a concise summary of Rosenblatt's theory and a warrant for its continued influence:

> Transactional theory offers a significantly different direction for moving beyond this deep division of reader and text. Applying a relational model developed in theory of knowledge and psychology to the study of literary experience, Louise M. Rosenblatt regards an aesthetic encounter with literature as temporal event, to which a reader and a text make an equal contribution. This is not, however, an equal exchange; in fact it is not an exchange at all. Rather, both reader and text join in a unified occasion: The poem is not an object but an experience, one in which reader and text join. It is an event that occurs in the time of experience, to which the reader brings knowledge, background, personality, and the skills of perception and comprehension to activate the ordered symbols of the text. This is probably the fullest development of the reader-response direction, one that comes closest to a complete integration of text and reader.[65]

In a transactional theory of literature, integration does not mean the absorption of either the text into the reader or the reader into the text. Distance between text and reader is essential to make space for what the reader brings to a text as well as the experiences and the reflections that are evoked from the *performance* of reading. Such distance fosters, rather than excludes, passionate emotional engagement as well as critical appreciation, reflection, and evaluation.

Distance in Rosenblatt's understanding of literature as *transaction* and *exploration* has significant implications for performance in general (and preaching in particular). Although Rosenblatt's transactional theory of literature discusses the importance of the reader in the event of the poem, it also draws significant parallels with the audience in the "event" of the performance of texts. She maintains that silent reading is a "performing art," where readers "perform in response to a text." She writes: "The reader performs the poem or the novel as the violinist performs the sonata. But the

65. Arnold Berleant, *Art and Engagement* (Philadelphia: Temple University Press, 1991), p. 121.

instrument on which the reader plays, and from which he evokes the work, is — himself." Rosenblatt then draws a correlation between reader and audience: the audience's response to a work performed is parallel to the reader's response to a text: "The listener makes meaning out of the sounds in a transactional process that parallels the reader's making meaning out of the visual text."[66] The transactional "two-way" relationship between the reader and text is the same dynamic in the two-way transaction between performer and audience whereby the audience becomes performer.

As in the case of the reader in relationship to the text, distance encourages and protects the responses of the hearer (emotions, criticism, passions, thoughts, judgments, rejections, and acceptances) as integral to the performance. As the reader is not passively absorbed into the text, neither is the hearer passively absorbed into the performance of a text (or a sermon). A transactional approach to performance transcends the text/reader–performer/hearer dichotomy whereby distance fosters not absorption but engagement.[67]

The basis of Rosenblatt's transactional theory is that literature is "exploration," "lived-through" experiences whereby the "reader seeks to participate in another's vision — to reap knowledge of the world, to fathom the resources of the human spirit, to gain insights that will make his own life more comprehensible." Such an exploration of literature that is dependent on the response of the reader changed her teaching from the deductive to the inductive method. She says that inductive methods of teaching "led me to differentiate between the old method, whereby leading questions were aimed at preordained conclusions, and my view, that 'the most fruitful inductive learning arises out of the involvement of the student . . . which leads him to raise personally meaningful questions . . . [and] to seek in the text the basis for valid answers and the impetus to further inquiry." She continues: "The problem that the teacher faces first of all, then, is the creation of a situation favorable to a vital experience of literature."[68] For Rosenblatt, the beginning of reading a text is the creation of space for the reader to hear, encounter, participate in, and inductively explore.

66. Rosenblatt, "Act 1, Scene 1: Enter the Reader," pp. 13, 21.

67. Berleant praises Rosenblatt's transactional understanding of literature as being closest to the direction he takes in *Art and Engagement*, p. 231.

68. Rosenblatt, *Literature as Exploration* (1976), pp. 7, ix-x, 61.

Backdrop for Preaching

When Fred Craddock introduced the term "distance" as part of his homiletical method in 1978, the concept had changed significantly from
Bullough's introduction of "psychical Distance" in 1912. For Bullough,
Distance was a universal aesthetic response that occurs when people psy-
chically remove themselves from a work of art or literature. This change in
perception is accomplished by perceivers suspending their personal interests, desires, feelings, and emotions, as well as any utilitarian or moral values they might be inclined to impose on the art object. Distance is obtained
by "separating the object and its appeal from one's own self by putting it
out of gear with practical needs and ends."[69] The goal of a true aesthetic
experience was a Kantian *disinterested contemplation,* whereby form was
appreciated for its balance and harmony, and beauty was enjoyed simply
for its own sake.

As universal claims in aesthetics were called into question, Bullough's
concept of Distance as an "aesthetic principle" was mainly abandoned by
the latter part of the twentieth century. What continued to develop, albeit
greatly transformed, was his observation of the function, or "dynamics,"
of Distance as a "factor in art." What originated in the philosophical field
of aesthetics as a principle became in performance studies and literary
criticism "distancing devices" and "techniques." Distance as an aesthetic
attitude, a dispassionate appreciation that was void of interest, emotion,
moral values, or utilitarian purposes, had become "devices" in an inductive
discovery by the reader/audience, whose purposes were complete engagement, passionate reflection, invested evaluation, emotional identification,
and ethical response. For speech-interpretation scholars such as Wallace
Bacon and Leland Roloff, the dynamics of distance protected the integrity
of both the text and the performer, preventing either one from being absorbed into the other. For presentational playwrights such as Thornton
Wilder, distancing techniques allowed the audience to see a drama as part
of something much "larger" than themselves, calling forth from the au-

---

69. Edward Bullough, "'Psychical Distance' as a Factor in Art and an Aesthetic
Principle," *The British Journal of Psychology* 5 (June 1912): 87-118, reprinted in Bullough,
Aesthetics: Lectures and Essays, p. 96.

dience wonder, mystery, and belonging. In Bertolt Brecht's epic theater, utilitarian function and ethical considerations were not stripped away but fostered as the primary purpose of performance. In these plays, intentional distancing devices, or "alienation effects," fostered both critical reflection and emotional participation. Being prompted to step backward, the reader or hearer could then step forward into a fuller engagement with the performance's significance to the greater community and the world. For literary critics like Louise Rosenblatt, distance becomes a negotiation between text and reader, whereby the reader's response becomes part of the "poem" via an inductive process of discovery. From these trajectories of distance in speech, theater, and literature, I return to my initial proposal: Distance between the audience and the performer, between the performer and the text, and between the text and the audience is integral to the *preservation of the text* and the *engagement of the hearer* in the *performance as an event.*

With this as a backdrop, we can now discuss the concept of distance in preaching.

CHAPTER THREE

Distance in Preaching:
Fred Craddock's Homiletical Method

As an enthusiast of literature, performance, and the art of storytelling, Fred Craddock clearly uses the dynamics and devices of aesthetic distance in his proposal of distance in preaching: a "psychical" separation, a "holding at bay" of the reader or audience from "direct participation" with a text or a performance through form, technique, style, and delivery. Distance fosters an inductive exploration of a text in which the reader becomes a performer, and the hearer is given the room or space to freely respond. Distance is an *approach* to a biblical text, dynamics *within* particular biblical texts, and intentional *tactics* in the creation, presentation, and delivery of a sermon. Echoing Wallace Bacon's metaphor of the dangerous shores of text and audience, Craddock says: "Because the term and idea of distance may need rehabilitation, I have urged that we think of distance as that quality in a communicative event that preserves invaluable benefits for the message and for the listener."[1]

In this chapter I will discuss Craddock's proposal of the "benefits" of distance for the message and the listener. Distance preserves the integrity of the biblical text, is theologically and morally warranted as a function of sermon style, is beneficial to the hearer, and thus should be used "intentionally" as a part of the sermon style and delivery.

---

1. Fred B. Craddock, *Overhearing the Gospel: Preaching and Teaching the Faith to Persons Who Have Heard It All Before* (Nashville: Abingdon, 1986), p. 121.

Preserving the Text: Distance in Interpretation

Beginning with the Hearer

With literature and performance as his backdrop, Craddock introduced distance to homiletics in his lectures entitled "Overhearing the Gospel: The Illusion of Truth without Imagination" (as the Lyman Beecher lecturer at Yale Divinity School for 1978). Those lectures were published later that year as *Overhearing the Gospel: Preaching and Teaching the Faith to Persons Who Have Heard It All Before.*[2] Influenced by the aforementioned literary and theatrical milieu of the time, Craddock adopted distance into homiletics by drawing on an eclectic variety of other sources: the hermeneutics of Paul Ricoeur and Hans Georg Gadamer, biblical scholars identified with the New Hermeneutic, the writing style of the nineteenth-century essayist Thomas de Quincey, the education theory of John Dewey, and the journals of Søren Kierkegaard. What is common in all these conversation partners is their high regard for the role of the hearer in the interpretation and performance of texts. Craddock's proposal of distance in preaching is based on a method of interpreting Scripture that begins with the hearer.

In his book *Theories of Preaching,* Richard Lischer categorizes Craddock's understanding of "distance and participation" under the heading of "rhetoric." Lischer notes that Craddock begins with the traditional concerns for the components of rhetoric: subject matter, speech-design, analysis of the hearer, and — I would add — the analysis of the speaker.[3] Before Craddock, rhetorical methods used by homileticians usually began with the message *(logos)*, or the speaker *(ethos)*, and proceeded to the listener *(pathos)*. The pastor's bookshelf of the time included homiletical textbooks that began with a message based on a text or topic, or with the character and spiritual disciplines of the speaker as preacher, pastor, and Christian. Only then did the reader proceed to the application of the sermon to the hearer as either the church at large or the person in the pew.

2. Fred B. Craddock, "Overhearing the Gospel: Illusion of Truth without Imagination," Parts 1 and 2, Lyman Beecher Lectures, Yale Divinity School, New Haven, Connecticut, 1978, cassette; published later that year as *Overhearing the Gospel* (n. 1 above).

3. Richard Lischer, *Theories of Preaching: Selected Readings in the Homiletical Tradition* (Durham, NC: Labyrinth Press, 1987), p. 250.

In white, mainline Protestant churches, this rhetorical progression from message to hearer was the legacy of the "Puritan Plain Style" or the "New Reformed Method" of preaching. William Perkins (1558-1602), in his homiletical handbook *The Art of Prophesying*, claimed the preacher's task was:

1. to read the text distinctly out of the canonical Scripture (excluding the Apocrypha);
2. to give the sense and understanding of the text according to the Scripture itself;
3. to collect a few and profitable points of doctrine out of the natural sense, avoiding allegorical and tropological senses;
4. to apply, "if he has the gift," these doctrines rightly collected to the life and manners of the congregation in a simple and plain speech.[4]

In Perkins's method of moving from Scripture to doctrine and then to the hearer, application to the life of the hearer was optional — depending on the ability of the preacher. The sermon was the Scripture text and the doctrinal message; the hearer was part of the sermon's application.

It must be noted that the rhetorical separation of the hearer from the sermon was not promoted by all homiletical traditions during Craddock's time. Two years before Craddock's address at Yale Divinity School, African-American homiletician Henry H. Mitchell, as the Lyman Beecher lecturer of 1974, spoke of the hearer's key role in black preaching:

> The recovery of preaching in America is heavily dependent on the willingness and ability of preachers to sit where their people sit, existentially and culturally. A working model of the effective communication of the gospel inside the life situation and common culture of the hearing folk is to be found in the preaching tradition of Blackamerican religion.

4. See Horton Davies, *Studies of the Church in History* (Allison Park, PA: Pickwick Publications, 1983), pp. 104-7; William Perkins, *The Art of Prophesying with The Calling of Ministry* (Edinburgh: Banner of Truth Trust, 1996; originally published in 1607); Joseph A. Pipa Jr., "William Perkins and the Development of Puritan Preaching" (PhD diss., Westminster Theological Seminary, 1985), text-fiche.

That tradition is examined here for what it may have to contribute to the American pulpit at large.[5]

Although Mitchell uses examples from black preaching specifically, he calls for the hearer's inclusion at the beginning of a homiletical method in order for preaching to be "recovered" in general in the American pulpit.

The precedence of the hearer in Mitchell's method is a progression from hearer to text as reflected in the chapter titles in *The Recovery of Preaching*. After "An Introductory Sermon," Mitchell begins by examining the hearer's context in "Preaching as 'Folk Culture.'" From there he moves to the role of emotion in "Preaching as Meaningful Personal Experience." He places the hearer in the context of worship in his discussion of "Preaching as Celebration"; but it is not until the middle of the book that he discusses the biblical text or the message (in the chapter entitled "Preaching as Storytelling"). Even then, the choice of story*telling* instead of simply *story* shows Mitchell's bias toward hearer participation.[6]

Similarly, Fred Craddock's own sequential move from hearer to text is reflected in the order of the chapters in his textbook *Preaching*. In the introduction, Craddock emphatically declares that preaching is both description and address, for both ingredients are necessary to the biblical witness. He says that "any narration of the story of Jesus must carry an implied if not expressed word of address to the listeners in order to qualify as preaching."[7] According to Craddock, any act of communication that speaks about God or Jesus but is not somehow addressed to the listener is not preaching. Unlike the legacy of Puritan plain preaching, Craddock does not reserve the hearer until the last step of application. Craddock's beginning point for sermon preparation and method of construction is made clear: "Preaching is to the listener intentionally" (pp. 17-18).

5. Henry H. Mitchell, *The Recovery of Preaching* (New York: Harper and Row, 1977), p. 11.

6. Mitchell, *The Recovery of Preaching*, pp. v, 74-95.

7. Fred B. Craddock, *Preaching* (Nashville: Abingdon, 1985), p. 18. Hereafter, page references to this work appear in parentheses in the text. Craddock's insistence that narration in the sermon must directly or indirectly address the hearer is the opposite of Mark Ellingsen's understanding of narrative in preaching. I will evaluate these differences in the discussion of postliberal homiletics in chap. 4.

After he includes the listener as part of the sermon by definition, he moves to "The Sermon in Context" in the next chapter:

> A sermon, to be properly understood and to have its purpose fulfilled, has to be experienced in its context, or rather in its several contexts. Such a statement could, of course, be aptly made regarding most events, but when it is made about a sermon, it is especially true in one respect. A sermon is a communication and therefore is to be located as much among a particular group of *listeners* as with a particular *speaker*. A knowledge of those to whom it is addressed would contribute as much or more to its understanding as would knowing the person who delivered it. And yet one seldom hears the inquiry, Who heard this sermon? Almost always the question is, Who preached this sermon? in spite of the fact that a sermon has many ears but only one mouth. (p. 31; italics added)

The context of the sermon is the historical, pastoral, liturgical, and theological context of the listener, which, for Craddock, is the person in the pew. Here again, the emphasis is on the "sermon's hearing."

After evaluating the contexts of the sermon's hearers, Craddock's next chapter moves to a "Theology of Preaching." Although such a move would be common in most preaching textbooks, what is unique about Craddock's approach is that he begins with "listening":

> In the consideration before us in this chapter, preaching is understood as making present and appropriate to the *hearers* the revelation of God. Here revelation is used not in the sense of content, although content is certainly there, but in the sense of mode. If preaching is in any way a continuation into the present of God's revelation, then what we are doing and how we are doing it should be harmonious with our understanding of the mode of revelation. At the risk of sounding presumptuous, it can be said that we are learning our method of communicating from God. (pp. 51-52; italics added)

As a theological warrant for his hearer-oriented method, Craddock says that the Word of God proceeds from "silence," is heard in a "whisper," and then is "shouted from the housetops" in preaching. Building on his understanding of communication in *Overhearing the Gospel*, Craddock makes it clear in *Preaching* that "shouting from the housetops" is not to be taken literally as a mode of preaching. As the Word of God is heard by the preacher, so the sermon is often heard in a "whisper" (pp. 51-60).

In what would appear to be a traditional move, Craddock proceeds to focus on the preacher in the next chapter, entitled "The Life of Study." However, where Craddock breaks with tradition is by emphasizing not the study of the Bible but of literature. Here again, the emphasis is on the hearer. When interviewed, Fred Craddock encouraged preachers to read at least fifteen minutes a day from a variety of literature, and especially plays. According to Craddock, this will not only give the preacher adept skills in language but, more importantly, will bring "new hearers" to the text by bringing into the pastor's study the "experiences of the person in the pew."[8] This is not to say that all reading material merits the preacher's time or attention. In a sermon, Craddock recalls a hospital visit where he sees a stack of magazines by the bed of a patient about to have major surgery. Bemoaning the steady diet of popular reading material, he says, "It occurred to me that there is not a calorie, in that whole stack, to help her through her experience. She had no place to dip down into a reservoir and come up with something."[9]

Craddock notes a benefit of reading good literature is that it "enlarges one's capacities as a creative human being and has a cumulative effect on one's vocabulary, use of the language, and powers of imagination. Not by conscious imitation but through the subtle influence of these great storytellers and poets, a preacher becomes more adept at arranging the materials of the sermon so that by restraint and thematic control, interest, clarity, and persuasiveness will be served" (*Preaching*, p. 79). All of literature's benefits to the preacher notwithstanding, Craddock makes it clear he does not promote its reading for the purpose of "usefulness" in a sermon. He describes combing through literature for illustrations as a "vulgar practice," and declares, "To read Flaubert for sermon illustrations would

8. Author interview of Fred B. Craddock, Columbia Theological Seminary, Decatur, Georgia, 1998.

9. Fred B. Craddock, "But If Someone Rises from the Grave," Mullins Lectures, Southern Baptist Theological Seminary, Louisville, Kentucky, 1987, cassette.

be prostitution" (pp. 78-79). During a question-and-answer period after a lecture he gave, an audience member asked, "Dr. Craddock, you seem well acquainted with contemporary literature. Do you read to be a better preacher?" Craddock replied, "No, I read to be a better human being."[10] Beneath Craddock's proposal to read literature as a part of a preacher's "Life of Study" is a concern for the hearer as a human being. Craddock promotes listening to a variety of human experiences, both inside and outside of the congregation. Through "empathetic imagination" with the person on the street and the person in the pew, the preacher brings to the text the ears of humanity — including those of the preacher (pp. 84-99).

After establishing *hearing* as the sermon's context and theological starting point, and *listening* as the "posture" of the pastor's life of study, Craddock does not approach "the text" until the middle of *Preaching*. In that chapter, where "Interpretation" is "Between Text and Listener," the hearer continues to be the focus (pp. 99-126). This approach of bringing "hearers" to a text has significant implications for creating and delivering sermons. In Craddock's method, the governing question for the preacher, "What shall I say?" must be accompanied by "What will be heard?"

In summary, where Craddock's method diverged from much of the white, mainline Protestant rhetorical tradition of his day was by beginning neither with the message *(logos)*, nor with the speaker *(ethos)*, but with the hearer *(pathos)*. In *Overhearing the Gospel*, Craddock observes: "It is so vital to our task that we be aware that the experience of listening is not a secondary consideration after we have done our exegesis of the texts and theological exploration. The *listener* is present from the beginning."[11] This does not mean that the listener is emphasized at the expense of the text. Craddock continues:

> The Christian tradition, biblical and extra-biblical, came to us from those who *heard* it, and we *hear* it and pass it on to other *hearers*. The stamp of listening and the listenability of the message is on it when we get it, and in telling it, we confirm that it is listenable. To give such

10. Craddock, Lecture at Candler School of Theology, Emory University, 1984.
11. Craddock, *Overhearing the Gospel*, p. 121 (italics added). Hereafter, page references to this work appear in parentheses in the text.

attention to the listener is not a concession to 'what they want to hear,' playing to the balcony or to the groundlings, nor is it an introduction to how to succeed as a speaker; it is no more or less than to describe the shape of the subject matter (it came from listeners) and the nature of the occasion (to effect a hearing). (p. 121; italics added)

In ways similar to Louise Rosenblatt's understanding of the reader as a part of the poem as "event," Craddock makes the hearer part of the occasion of the biblical text. Hearers originally "occasion" the creation of the text, and contemporary hearers occasion its hearing for today.

Overhearing the Biblical Text: Preserving the Message

Craddock establishes the *experience of listening* as the "governing consideration in a communicative event" and the "preoccupation that harnesses the imaginative, emotive, and cognitive powers of the speaker" (p. 121). He characterizes the posture of listening, what he calls "overhearing," as being comprised of two elements: *distance* and *participation*. In *Overhearing the Gospel*, he proposes that distance be integral to the "overhearing" of biblical texts and the gospel, and thereby warranted for intentional use in the sermon's construction and hearing. Here he proposes a method of interpreting biblical texts that preserves the distance necessary for their integrity as historical documents, and at the same time fosters the participation necessary so that they may function as "Scripture" in the faith and life of the church today. Craddock identifies this method as *overhearing*. Drawing on the field of aesthetics, Craddock notes that overhearing Scripture is like overhearing a musical performance, a play, or reading a good book, for its power is due to the dynamic of two factors: distance and participation. Whether one is overhearing a performance or Scripture, Craddock describes the hearer's experience of distance as "I am an anonymous listener, reader, viewer, unrelated to the event"; and he describes a *participator* as "I am drawn in by identification with persons and conditions within the event" (p. 121; italics added).

For Craddock, the two components of any good communication, distance and participation, meet us "immediately and unavoidably" when the

54

Bible is read or heard. Participation is intrinsic to the nature of the Bible when we approach it as the "church's scripture," the "living Word," and the "norm for faith and life." Yet a temporal distance between the reader and the text is also obvious when the reader is confronted with strange language, remote places, and unfamiliar names. Craddock notes that, though such distance may pose a problem for any serious reader of the Bible, it also serves as a "blessing," for distance preserves the integrity of the Christian faith against any tendency "to sacrifice and consume the past by any reader insisting on an immediate and relevant word at this moment" (p. 61).

In his understanding of "overhearing" a biblical text (or, for that matter, a sermon), Craddock agrees with William Beardslee that distance serves as a safeguard against "mystic identification," whereby the text is either absorbed into the consciousness of the reader or the reader is somehow absorbed into the world of the text. As I have suggested in chapter 2 above, Bertolt Brecht warned that complete identification of an audience member with a character is at the expense of the play's greater meaning. Similarly, Beardslee prefers *conversation* to *identification* in order to protect the meaning of the text. In conversation, the text's integrity is preserved through distance as a part of *dialogue* (pp. 114-16).[12] This is not to say that Craddock is against imaginative participation with a text. On the contrary, full participation comes from a combination of identification with the characters in the text and a dialogue with a text. In contrast to Beardslee, Craddock's approach of "overhearing" a biblical text preserves distance in both identification and conversation, leading the reader or hearer to a fuller participation with a text.

While Craddock promotes a posture in which the reader overhears rather than hears a text, he clarifies that he does not intend to minimize the direct hearing of biblical texts. He credits Karl Barth and Rudolf Bultmann with recovering the "Word of God" as "direct address to us" during a time when the history-of-religions approach dominated (especially) New Testament interpretation. Craddock describes the history-of-religions approach, with its focus on objectivity and pure description, as responsible for a "total lack of advocacy" for the interpreter, preacher, and hearer.[13]

12. Craddock builds on the work of William A. Beardslee, *Literary Criticism of the New Testament* (Philadelphia: Fortress, 1970), esp. pp. 10-13.

13. Fred B. Craddock, "Recent New Testament Interpretation and Preaching," *Princeton Seminary Bulletin* 66, no. 1 (October 1973): 80.

Although this approach allowed the scholar to talk *about* a text, it did little to assist the preacher in the preparation and proclamation of a sermon to be heard in today's world. According to Craddock, by turning the "face of the text" directly toward us, Barth and Bultmann fostered confrontational theology and existential interpretations that enlivened both biblical scholarship and preaching.[14]

While acknowledging the contributions of Barth and Bultmann to preaching, Craddock is critical of Bultmann's legacy for fostering sermons that "pressed" for a decision from their hearers through the sole use of direct address. He credits Bultmann's methods of biblical interpretation as setting free the "Word of God as address," in order to effect for the listener "the unmediated existential encounter."[15] Yet, according to Craddock, defining the Word of God as address contracted the experience of the hearer to a decision. By reducing the hearer to a "decider," confrontation gave no room for the "happy accident of overhearing." As Craddock says, " 'Once upon a time' capitulated to 'once for all' " (*Overhearing*, p. 118).

Craddock argues that, if preaching is to be a word that speaks to the many facets of human experience, as well as being faithful to the biblical text, then direct address as the only mode of communication is not adequate on both accounts. Craddock quotes Amos Wilder: "The Word of God is more than address just as I am more than volition."[16] As life is multidimensional, so the relationship between the text and listener cannot be exclusively one of confrontation and decision. In further support of his argument, Craddock notes that, though some biblical texts are direct and confrontational by nature, many are not. In order for us to be faithful to a variety of texts, he proposes that "it is more appropriate to some texts to overhear them rather than to hear them."[17]

---

14. Craddock, "Recent New Testament Interpretation," pp. 79-81.

15. Craddock, *Overhearing*, p. 117; Fred Craddock, *As One Without Authority* (St. Louis: Chalice Press, 2001), pp. 40-42.

16. Amos Wilder, "The Word as Address and the Word as Meaning," in James Robinson and John Cobb, eds., *The New Hermeneutic: New Frontiers in Theology*, vol. 2 (New York: Harper and Row, 1964), cited by Craddock in "Recent New Testament Interpretation," p. 79.

17. Craddock, "Recent New Testament Interpretation," p. 79.

Overhearing the Argument: Distance and Polemics

Craddock notes that one tool of interpretation that calls for distance is the overhearing of an argument or conflict in biblical texts. Here Craddock draws on Ernst Käsemann's analysis of New Testament texts in terms of polemics. Unlike a confrontational approach, where the polemic would be between the text and the reader, Käsemann's polemic is between two parties within a text. As an example, Craddock presents the debate in 2 Corinthians 10–13 as the tension between two types of apostolic ministry:

> Into the Corinthian congregations came certain "superlative apostles" who had strong letters of recommendation and who underscored their ministry with wondrous deeds and mighty works. Such men turned many heads. On the other hand, there was the founding father, Paul. His letters of recommendation? The Corinthian Christians themselves. His boast of mighty works? His boast was what he suffered, what he had endured, his weaknesses through which God's strength was perfected. The Corinthians must decide what constitutes authentic apostolic ministry.[18]

How Craddock sets up the argument is a prime example of his method and style not only in his interpretation of texts but also in his sermons. Overhearing in contrast to hearing comes through in the use of indirect rather than direct address. Instead of directly addressing the hearer with an immediate defense of Paul and a predictable scourge of the Corinthians, Craddock gives us the distance to stand back, weigh the issues, and listen to both sides as the two parties address each other. The benefit is that the hearer is drawn in slowly after reevaluating the nature of Christian ministry and the workings of God in the world. Through the gradual overcoming of distance by providing room for honest evaluation, participation is more faithful to the issues and questions raised by the text.

Not all polemics are arguments between persons or groups. Overhearing a polemic may also pertain to the tension between theological perspec-

---

18. Craddock, "Recent New Testament Interpretation," p. 80. The reader is reminded that the quote is from a lecture where Craddock's delivery would have drawn out the argument within the text.

tives. Craddock notes Theodore Weeden's proposal to read the Gospel of Mark as a "dramatic presentation of two Christologies."[19] In this drama, Jesus presents the Messiah as one who serves and suffers, whereas his disciples insist on the Messiah as the "Divine Man" who works miracles and overcomes all obstacles. In Mark, both images are in conflict and create a "double image" of Christ. Following Craddock's method, a *direct* hearing of the Marcan text would attempt to resolve the tension too quickly by choosing one "image" over the other. Aesthetician Edward Bullough observes that new understanding takes place when distance is negotiated with participation and slowly overcome. The goal for a work of art is to obtain the least amount of distance necessary for participation, yet at the same time to preserve adequate space for reflection, contemplation, and evaluation. Similarly, Craddock encourages the reader to draw near enough to overhear, while at the same time keeping the distance necessary to question and evaluate his or her own images of the Christ and discipleship. When this tension between distance and participation is obtained, "overhearing becomes hearing."[20]

Overhearing the Characters: Distance and Identification

When we approach a text, distance creates "space" or "room" for evaluating a text through self-evaluation. One way we can accomplish this is to prevent facile or false identifications with biblical characters. Craddock gives as an example the conflict between Jesus and the Pharisees. Whether the debate is over forgiveness, eating with sinners, fasting, keeping the Sabbath, or divorce, a too hasty identification with Jesus can reduce the Pharisees to caricatures. When we flatten the Pharisees as characters to the point of no longer being believable, we lose the believability of Jesus and his mission as well.

This back and forth movement from distance to identification is especially prominent in Craddock's method of interpreting parables. In his

19. Theodore Weeden, *Mark: Traditions in Conflict* (Philadelphia: Fortress, 1972), as quoted in Craddock, "Recent New Testament Interpretation," p. 80.
20. Craddock, "Recent New Testament Interpretation," p. 80.

commentary on Luke 15:1-32, titled "Three Parables of Joy," Craddock begins by giving the hearer "room" for self-reflection as the receiver of the story. He says:

> Before moving to the parables themselves, the reader will want to take a moment to consider where he or she is sitting while receiving the stories. Is it beside Jesus, as though joining Jesus in addressing these parables to critics, or is it among those being addressed by Jesus? In texts in which Jesus is facing opponents, we who deal with these texts can so easily, but certainly not intentionally, preach and teach them as the voice of Jesus rather than as those who need to hear the voice of Jesus.

Distance increases when Craddock goes on to say that questioning where and who we are in the parable does not mean "we must label ourselves Pharisees and scribes." Yet distance decreases as direct address increases: "[B]ut it does mean we realize that these texts were written not simply out of historical interest in the religious community surrounding Jesus but primarily because these texts address a church with the problems herein associated with Pharisees and scribes. There is no room to say, 'I thank thee I am not as they were.'" Although Jesus did not force an immediate identification between the hearer and the Pharisees and scribes, Craddock is not ready to rule out that such identification may exist. The result is an unresolved tension between distance and identification.

Craddock then proceeds to justify the Pharisees' point of view according to Old Testament laws and community responsibility. After an honest attempt to "stand beside" the Pharisees, he comes to rest by another group: "Perhaps the most fitting location for us, then, is not with Jesus or with the Pharisees but among tax collectors and sinners, who find ourselves welcomed and forgiven in his presence." With this final identification with "those addressed by Jesus," distance is diminished but not overcome due to previous identifications with different perspectives within the text.[21]

Identification does not necessarily mean the diminishing of distance. Sometimes the artifice of total identification with a character or an as-

21. Fred B. Craddock, *Luke* (Louisville: Westminster John Knox Press, 1990), pp. 184-85.

sumed character in the story can create distance. In the sermon "Can I Also Be Included?" Craddock invites the congregation to overhear the text by taking on the perspective of one of its characters. Without previous introduction to the congregation, he begins the sermon by setting the scene:

> To the text for today. It involves one of those church meetings that we, most of us, I think, hate to attend; not in spite of the fact that it was a *church* meeting, but because it was a church *meeting*. Church meetings can be the most incendiary of all. We knew it was going to be rough. It was a called meeting. We knew it was going to be rough because the notice said, "Everyone select delegates" for the meeting. We knew it was going to be rough when we got to the room and found a note under the door, "Will the Antioch Delegation meet thirty minutes before the plenary." And then, arriving in the great hall, it looked like a forest of microphones. It is going to be confrontational. I don't do well in that kind of setting. I'd rather go shopping and then come back and say, "How did it go? I wish I'd have been there."
>
> It was a single-issue meeting. Luke says it was a single-issue meeting. The issue? Clear. Are we going to continue to admit into full standing and fellowship in the church, foreigners?[22]

Instead of explaining the conflict in Luke regarding the inclusion of the Gentile converts, Craddock allows the congregation to overhear the conflict by addressing them as one of the delegates to the "church meeting." He takes on a character, and as he does so, the direct address of the delegate to the congregation becomes the indirect address of the preacher. The benefit of this technique is that the hearer can be directly addressed without necessarily being threatened. The space given at the beginning through the artifice of a character leads to what Craddock calls "the shock of recognition" by the end of the sermon regarding God's call — and thus the church's call — to welcome.[23] Craddock continues in character:

22. Fred B. Craddock, "Can I Also Be Included?" Lecture at Candler School of Theology, Emory University, Atlanta, Georgia, Nov. 14, 1985, cassette (oral emphasis added).

23. Fred B. Craddock, "Preaching and the Shock of Recognition," Hickman Lectures, Duke Divinity School, Durham, North Carolina, Oct. 30, 1984, cassette.

Whose fault is it? I mean, here the church is doing fine, started off with thousands and thousands, multiplied and spread out from Jerusalem and it is just doing great and we got little congregations in all the towns and then this! It is just going to split us wide open, and then what's going to happen? Just when everything was going so well. You know whose fault I think it is? I think it is Stephen's. When he made that speech against the temple in Jerusalem, that's what started it. Now he was appointed to wait tables, but he thought he had to preach. Everybody wants to preach, and that's what started it. [Pause] No, I don't think so, I think it is Philip. You know, he went up there and let those be baptized, some of those Samaritans, he baptized some of those Samaritans, and when you let those Samaritans in, the camel's nose is in the tent. [Pause] Well, no, I really, I really think it is Simon Peter. He doesn't want us to know about it, but I happened to know because I have a sister that lives in Caesarea; he ate with some Italians. Yeah, yeah, the word is out. The word is out. We're supposed to think of him as one of our leaders, an apostle. Isn't it really, though, the fault of Paul, running around here, claiming this vision, claiming to be an apostle to the Gentiles and just — he just takes in everybody. He just lets them all in. Yeah, yeah, y'all come. And look at his churches. Holding their bulletins upside down, don't know an introit from a benediction. He just lets in everybody and that's when it all turns sour, as far as I am concerned. [Pause] No, I don't think so. I really think it was Barnabas. Bless his heart, he is such a fine person, but you know how we'd all agreed in Jerusalem. If Paul ever shows up here he can fellowship with us, he can take the Lord's table with us, but he is not to preach. Oh, he can have the benediction or something. He is not to preach. But Barnabas took him around, and worked him in, and, pretty soon, there he is preaching. Now Barnabas should not have done that — he knows better. Whose fault is it? Luke says — [Pause] — Luke says, the fault is God's. That God sent the Holy Spirit to push and shove the church, pushed and shoved the church, beyond ethnic borders, national borders, social borders, economic borders, that repentance and forgiveness be preached to all nations.[24]

24. Craddock, "Can I Also Be Included?"

According to previously discussed categories in performance theory, observe that Craddock's method of performance is not "representational" but "presentational." He does not ask that we forget he is Fred Craddock in the twentieth century through the use of prop or costume. Nor does he try to re-create the setting of Antioch in the first century. On the contrary, Craddock intentionally uses devices such as Southern colloquialisms ("church meeting") and anachronism ("forest of microphones") to distance the hearer from the story and its teller, allowing the hearer to participate with a "willing suspension of disbelief." This is what Craddock refers to as "overhearing" the story. We are not asked to step fully into the text's story by suspending our own; nor is the biblical story absorbed into our story. Through overhearing we are given room or space to listen to the biblical story as it might speak to us today.

Instead of a direct address demanding that a congregation expand its boundaries, Craddock's indirect approach in the above sermon allows the hearers to drop their guard. For Craddock, a benefit of overhearing is that it is "nonthreatening." Noting human nature, Craddock observes that when threatened the hearer does not think, listen, ponder, reflect, or decide because all the faculties are "lined up along the barricades in anxious defense." Instead of confronting the hearer with a text like a javelin, overhearing allows the listener to be "free to think, to feel, to resolve."[25]

Craddock compares overhearing Scripture to attending a play, where listeners are permitted "to hear the responsibility for their own participation." Discoveries about oneself and identifications are made as the hearer is not forced but *permitted* to be drawn into the action. He says: "The air is not filled with ought, must, and should, and yet imperatives are felt and cannot be shaken when the curtain falls. In a real sense, permission to draw conclusions about life is a demand to do so." As Craddock reminds us, "it is the possibility of a No that makes the Yes a real Yes."[26]

By delivering the sermon as a possible character in the biblical story, the preacher is not "using a text" to address a congregation directly. In-

25. Craddock, "Recent New Testament Interpretation," p. 81.
26. Craddock, "Recent New Testament Interpretation," p. 81. For a further discussion of the role of the hearer's resistance in the sermon as being a part of the sermon's acceptance, see James E. Dittes, *When the People Say No: Conflict and the Call to Ministry* (San Francisco: Harper and Row, 1979).

stead, overhearing that includes distance as well as participation calls for a trust in the power of a biblical text to effect change in the life of a hearer, while at the same time it considers the listener's response.

Hermeneutical Distance: Protecting the Text

We have seen in Craddock's theory and sermons that distance as a part of overhearing allows a polemic within a text to be heard on its own terms, protects the text from a too easy identification with biblical characters, and trusts the power of the text's message by giving the hearers room and responsibility for their own response. In these examples the "benefit of distance" for a text is also a fuller participation or engagement by the hearer.

But Craddock has been challenged by the claim that, by "beginning with the hearer," his method of interpretation is at the "expense of the biblical story."[27] Although Craddock rhetorically begins with the listener's approach to a text, he emphatically declares that it is not at the expense, meaning, or integrity of the text as a work *outside* the listener. He is not proposing overhearing as absorption of the text into the reader's response. For Craddock, quite the opposite is true:

> For the message, distance preserves its objectivity as history, its continuity as tradition, and its integrity as a word that has existence prior to and apart from me as a listener. In other words, the distance between the message and the listener conveys the sense of the substantive nature and independence of the message, qualities that add to rather than detract from the persuasive and attention-drawing power of the message.[28]

27. Author interview of Charles Lamar Campbell, Columbia Theological Seminary, Decatur, Georgia, 1998. See also Campbell, *Preaching Jesus: New Directions for Homiletics in Hans Frei's Postliberal Theology* (Grand Rapids: Eerdmans, 1997).

28. Craddock, *Overhearing the Gospel*, p. 121; see also chapters 4 and 5 of that book, "Concerning the Story" (pp. 57-78) and "Recent New Testament Interpretation" (pp. 78-81). Regarding the function of distance as a preservation of the autonomy of the text, Craddock has been influenced by the hermeneutics of Paul Ricoeur. Craddock cites Ricoeur, "Biblical Hermeneutics," *Semeia* 4 (1975): 29-148. Ricoeur develops his function of distance further in "The Hermeneutical Function of Distanciation," in *Hermeneutics and the Human Sciences: Essays on Language, Action, and Interpretation,*

In Craddock's method, distance provides invaluable benefits for the message by identifying and protecting the *separation* between the reader and the text. In the presentation of a case study of his method for sermon preparation, he describes the importance of the role of distance when we study a biblical text. Here he summarizes his hermeneutic of distance:

> In order to study there must be respect for sufficient distance for one to see and hear clearly. Distance between preacher and text, between preachers and listeners, and between text and listeners is not simply a historical, sociological and psychological fact grudgingly recognized. Distance can be fruitful for honest understanding, and also exciting as preacher and listeners grow in anticipation of negotiating that distance in the process for the sermon itself. In an age that puts a premium on immediate intimacy, distance has lost respect. The preacher will need to beware of collapsing distances too quickly in the haste to achieve for the listeners instant relevance and intimacy in relation to the ancient text. Otherwise, the result can be a smothering of both text and listener.

Craddock's claim is that distance, when recognized at the beginning of the study of a text, preserves the integrity of text, preacher, and listener. He goes on to say that, when distance is first recognized and then respected, it can be bridged in the sermon via *analogy* and *points of identification*.[29]

Because of the preacher's strong desire to be responsible to and for the congregation before her, and at the same time not be discontinuous with the biblical text or the church that brought it to her, Craddock proposes that the preacher welcome the "new angle of vision" among New Testament interpreters who speak of the "future of the text" or the "for-

---

ed. and trans. John B. Thompson (New York: Cambridge University Press, 1981). Craddock's "distance" differs from Ricoeur's "distanciation" in that Craddock emphasizes the distance between the hearer and the text, whereas Ricoeur emphasizes the process of distanciation among text, author, and original context. For Ricoeur, distanciation occurs when a created work is read or heard, whereby it becomes "decontextualized" from its creator as well as the social and historical conditions of its creation. The result is new meaning from new perspectives and unrestrictive readings.

29. Craddock, "Occasion-Text-Sermon: A Case Study," *Interpretation* 35, no. 1 (January 1981): 60-61.

ward movement of the text."[30] With a hermeneutic that perceives a text as "forward movement," the preacher does not abandon critical tools and hermeneutical questions, but uses them as what Craddock calls "servants of the Word." Critical tools help the "reader" of Scripture understand how the "soil" of each new situation becomes "ingredient to the new telling and hearing of the story."[31]

In contrast to both positivism, a description of the past without regard for the present, and existentialism, a dissolving of the past into the present, Craddock's understanding of a text "moving forward" neither eliminates distance nor does it relieve its tension. He says: "When the text ceases to be a story mediating revelation and meaning, the reaction is to dismiss the past and 'sink into the warm stream of the immediate.'"[32] With the preservation of distance, both the integrity of the past and the integrity of the present are maintained, since future interpretation is included in the nature of the text. Craddock suggests that "the sermon does not simply look back to the text; it fulfills the text." The result is that the preacher can approach the text "anticipating meaning," and knowing that her or his "interest" is part of an "acceptable hermeneutical principle."[33]

Summary

In summary, distance functions in Craddock's method as both a hermeneutical principle and an interpretive tool. Although Craddock's interpretive method for preaching begins with a strong consideration of the hearer's participation, I have shown how his use of distance as a part of

30. Craddock credits the phrases "future of the text" and "forward movement of the text" to Robert Funk in *Language, Hermeneutic and the Word of God: The Problem of Language in the New Testament and Contemporary Theology* (New York: Harper and Row, 1966), pp. 124-223.

31. Craddock, "Recent New Testament Interpretation," pp. 77-78.

32. Craddock, *Overhearing*, p. 76, quoting Stephen Crites, "The Narrative Quality of Experience," *Journal of American Academy of Religion* 39 (September 1971): 310.

33. Craddock, "Recent New Testament Interpretation," p. 78. Craddock attributes "interest" and "anticipation of meaning" as a hermeneutical principle to Robert Funk in *Language, Hermeneutics and the Word of God*, and to Peter Hodgson, *Jesus — Word and Presence* (Philadelphia: Fortress, 1971), pp. 31-48.

overhearing safeguards the text's integrity against "absorption" by the reader or hearer. As Craddock says, "Overhearing is a method of appropriating and communicating Scripture that preserves the distance from the text necessary to its own integrity as an historical document and the participation in the text necessary to its faith and life function as the Scripture of the church today" (*Overhearing*, p. 115).

I have also demonstrated that Craddock's use of distance, when used as an interpretive tool, preserves conflict within the text from easy resolutions and protects biblical characters from being flattened by facile identifications or rejections from the reader/hearer. By protecting the text's conflict, reversal, offense, or surprise, distance prevents an easy dismissal *by* the hearer of an uneasy message intended *for* the hearer. When these dynamics are protected and preserved through distance, their aim is to "effect a new hearing" for the preacher and for the congregation. The means by which these dynamics have their "effect" are elements of style.

Protecting the Hearer: Distance in the Sermon

Distance as Style

How Craddock moves from distance as an interpretive tool when approaching a biblical text to its use as a device in the creation and delivery of a sermon is based on his understanding of distance as an element of style. Essential for Craddock's defense of distance is the essential nature of style to the communication of the gospel in Scripture and sermon. In *Preaching*, Craddock observes:

> Preaching is understood as making present and appropriate to the hearers the revelation of God. Here revelation is used not in the sense of content, although content is certainly there, but in the sense of mode. If preaching is in any way a continuation into the present of God's revelation, then what we are doing and how we are doing it should be harmonious with our understanding of the mode of revelation. At the risk of sounding presumptuous, it can be said that we are learning our method of communicating from God. (*Preaching*, pp. 51-52)

In *Overhearing the Gospel*, Craddock identifies and discusses the "how" of communicating and continuing God's revelation as *style*. The style in which revelation is communicated in Scripture should inform the style in which revelation continues through preaching. Craddock argues that style is an integral and moral component in the communication of the Christian message in sermon text and delivery: "It is not to be assumed that the gospel provides religious and moral constraints upon *what* we say but leaves *how* we say it to be governed solely by practical considerations of effectiveness. This simply is not true" (*Overhearing*, p. 20). For Craddock, style is part of the "very fabric of the occasion, of the relationship, of an event, of the truth" of preaching (*Overhearing*, pp. 19-20).

In this section I will present Craddock's proposal for the reclaiming of distance as a stylistic device of indirect speech for the purpose of overhearing the gospel. After providing a general working definition of sermon style, I will discuss Craddock's integral relationship between sermon style and content, his intentional use of distancing devices as modeled by Scripture and literature, and his particular emphasis on the oral and kinesthetic function of distance in sermon delivery.

Although the last two chapters of *Preaching* and most of *Overhearing the Gospel* are dedicated to matters of *style* in communication and preaching, Craddock neither defines nor clarifies the term. Mary E. Lyons provides a definition and description of sermon style that is helpful in clarifying Craddock's proposal. She says that *style* as a characteristic of a sermon's text is its "texture and design."[34] Lyons explains that a treatment of preaching style in its broadest sense would consider its place within the dynamics of the preacher, the assembly, and the texts of Scripture and sermon. Lyons notes that from these dynamics a discussion of the characteristics of preaching style would involve "who and how one speaks; who hears and how they listen; what is spoken and in what space and for what occasion."[35]

34. Mary E. Lyons, "Style," in William H. Willimon and Richard Lischer, eds., *Concise Encyclopedia of Preaching* (Louisville: Westminster John Knox, 1995).

35. Lyons's "dynamics" of preaching style as involving speaker, audience, setting, and occasion could also be seen as categories of rhetoric. Although Craddock addresses these dynamics in his works on preaching, he generally prefers the term "style" rather than "rhetoric." One exception is his article entitled "Is There Still Room for Rheto-

While recognizing these general dynamics of preaching style, Lyons restricts her focus in particular to the "artifact" of preaching, the sermon text read or delivered orally. Pertinent to Craddock's emphasis on a preaching style that is to "effect a hearing," Lyons says that "the principal element of a sermon's style is its language, the words and sentences selected by the author, their arrangement or distortion in order to produce some *effect upon the hearer.*" Lyons notes that every sermon, whether uttered spontaneously, written in advance, or transcribed after delivery, reveals through its composition "textures and designs" that can be named and evaluated.[36] These textures and designs of language and their effect on the hearer in delivery make up a sermon's style.

Focusing on the sermon text, Lyons identifies the two major components of sermon style as being "figures of speech" and "figures of thought": "When crafted well, the sermon is always a memorable discourse composed of figures and moves that do not call attention to themselves; rather they advance the preacher's intention. Consciously or not, preachers depend upon certain figures of speech and thought in order to create their desired effect." Lyons describes the distinction between figures of thought and figures of speech: "figures of speech are semantic distortions designed for effect; figures of thought are syntactic arrangements for the same purpose."[37]

Lyons's definition and description provides a helpful vocabulary for Craddock's understanding of distance as a component of sermon style. In Lyons's vocabulary, distance as a characteristic and device of sermon style would be a distortion or disruption in the arrangement of the sermon's texture and design in order to produce an effect on the hearer. More specifically, distance would function like a figure of speech, a semantic distortion designed for its effect.

---

ric?" where he expresses reservations about rhetoric's legacy of reducing the sermon to persuasion that is accomplished through a single form of deductive reasoning. In his rejection of coercion as congruent with a "Christian style" of communication, he is wary of any forms of persuasion from a "bully pulpit" that silences other voices and views. While cautious, Craddock affirms those who are making a "broader reappropriation of rhetoric" through the inclusion of poetics. See Fred B. Craddock, "Is There Still Room for Rhetoric?" in Martha F. Simmons, ed., *Preaching on the Brink: The Future of Homiletics* (Nashville: Abingdon, 1996), pp. 66-74.

36. Lyons, "Style."
37. Lyons, "Style."

Craddock's proposal of distance as a characteristic of style modifies Lyons's definition in three areas. The first is with regard to the relationship between style and delivery. Although Lyons says that style refers to the sermon text as "read or spoken orally," she ignores the connection between written and oral characteristics of style. What remains is the *intent* to have an effect on the hearer by means of the structure and language of the text. What is omitted is the text's performance through its style by means of its delivery. This neglect of delivery runs contrary to Craddock's proposal of the sermon being an acoustical event, arising from oral speech and returning to oral speech. As I will discuss later in this chapter, Craddock's case for distance as a function of overhearing and indirect communication involves not only written but also vocal, visual, and kinesthetic style.

A second area in which Craddock's proposal revises Lyons's description regards her list of the "characteristics of style." Added to "figures of thought" and "figures of speech" would be the "figures of the speaker," the persona of the preacher in relationship to the biblical text, the sermon text, and the hearer. Examples of such narrative devices have been previously identified in excerpts of Craddock sermons. They include the indirect telling of stories by trying on the different perspectives of biblical characters, approaching the text as a potential hearer (from both inside and outside the congregation), and speaking in the voice of biblical characters (stated or imagined) through extended role-plays.

In light of Craddock's proposal for overhearing and indirect speech, a third area requiring revision is Lyons's "aims of style." She observes that preachers usually choose to "texture" their sermon for one of three reasons: to advance, to emphasize, or to amplify. Although the skilled preacher can draw on any number of stylistic devices, Lyons proposes that "no matter how plain or how grand the style, sermons embody devices that aim at one or more of those ends."[38] According to Craddock's proposal for overhearing, in order to *advance*, the hearer may require the preacher to "hold at bay," to de-emphasize through indirect speech, to reduce and pull back — that is, to *distance*.

38. Lyons, "Style."

Distance as Overhearing and Indirect Address

> The distinguishing characteristic in life is not what is said
> but how it is said.
>
> Søren Kierkegaard[39]

In *Overhearing the Gospel*, Craddock's underlying question for the discussion of preaching is: How does one person communicate the Christian faith to another? Craddock notes that such a question may be problematic, because "how" is for many an "ugly word," and "cause for embarrassment."[40] Addressing his audience in 1978, he says that the "large opinion" of the time is that "how" is to be found "not among the prophets or the philosophers but among mechanics and carpenters." He rhetorically asks: "After all, does not 'how' introduce methods and skills more appropriate to a course in driver training than to probing into the mysteries of ultimate reality? What does skill have to do with the kingdom of God?" (p. 10)

Craddock argues that a significant factor contributing to the decline of the quality of preaching in his time is the inattention and disregard for "how" for the sake of "what." He observes: "'How' has been made to stand out in the hall while 'What' was being entertained by the brightest minds among us. *What* is the issue? *What* is the truth? *What* do we believe? *What* is being taught? Those are the worthy questions, and who would suffer the embarrassment of interrupting the discussion with 'but how can we . . . ?'" (p. 10) Craddock blames this arrogant dismissal of "how" mainly on the academy, where sermon method, form, and style have been neglected in favor of the sermon's content or message. The result is the "paralysis" of new ministers in the pulpit who know "what" they want to say, but do not know "how" to communicate it to their congregations.

According to Craddock, in the homiletics of his time, "how" had been separated from "what," "manner" from "matter," and "style" from "con-

---

39. Søren Kierkegaard, *Journals*, X^2, A, p. 466, quoted in Craddock, *Overhearing*, p. 80.

40. Craddock, *Overhearing*, p. 10. Hereafter, page references to this work appear in parentheses in the text.

tent" (pp. 10-17). The result is a "severing" of the hearer from the sermon and the gospel: "And those of us concerned to communicate the Christian gospel, while confessing to the intrinsic adequacy of the message for salvation, must all the while follow the operational principle, *if it has been heard*" (p. 16; italics in original). As a biblical text without a hearer no longer functions as Scripture, so, for Craddock, a sermon severed from the hearer no longer functions as the proclamation of the gospel. Craddock stakes his claim that the justification of sermon style is to "effect a hearing of the gospel"; yet he admits that to effect that hearing is no small task (p. 16).

A significant part of *Overhearing the Gospel* is a discussion of a sermon style that is "fitting" in order to effect a hearing of the gospel. In the final chapter Craddock expresses this primary consideration for the hearer in his method of interpreting biblical texts and preaching. He declares that such a consideration is neither concession (saying what they want to hear) nor utilitarian (how to succeed as a speaker). Craddock's emphasis on the hearer is based on the shape of the subject matter (it came from listeners) and the nature of the occasion (to effect a hearing). His proposal is as follows: "Having begun with the experience of listening as the governing consideration in a communicative event and as the preoccupation that harnesses the imaginative, emotive, and cognitive powers of the speaker, I characterized that posture of listening called overhearing as consisting of two elements: distance and participation" (p. 121). In Craddock's proposal, distance functions as a "posture" of overhearing, a "natural, effective, and at times life-changing dynamic" that belongs in the sermon and pulpit (p. 120).

Craddock diagnoses two maladies of preaching during his time: the first is the separation of style from content; the second follows from the first — that familiarity with the Christian message is the same as living out the Christian faith. According to the second, matters of communication are no longer necessary because the congregation is already familiar with the church's stories and doctrines. According to Craddock, the symptoms of both maladies have been dull, information-oriented sermons with little consideration for the hearer.[41]

---

41. I would remind the reader that when Craddock speaks of the "congregation"

Craddock attacks these "illusions" of contemporary preaching by stating his conviction concerning the aims of the church and its proclamation:

> We have no more urgent or important or demanding task than that of effecting a *new hearing* of the gospel. Communication is not a second and optional field subordinate to Bible or theology or church history or parish administration. Christianity, whether in broad perspective or narrow assignment, is communication. (p. 79; italics added)

A call for a "new" hearing is not to negate or offer judgment on previous hearings; rather, it emphasizes that the gospel is to be heard "ever anew" by hearers in new times and places. Craddock admits that the gospel receiving a new hearing in the present context is a condition "most difficult by its having been heard before," and a challenge that "taxes all faculties of thought and imagination" (pp. 79-81).

After diagnosing the maladies of preaching according to its "illusions," and then challenging these illusions with the aims of preaching, Craddock proposes a remedy: "overhearing." According to Craddock, overhearing is a method of appropriating and communicating Scripture that is both faithful to the message of the gospel and effective for its communication. In preaching, overhearing is attained through indirect address in sermon style and delivery. Indirect address uses distance as a dynamic between biblical text, sermon, preacher, and hearer, and as a technique of sermon style and delivery. In Craddock's proposal, distance is both a *dynamic* and a *device* for the purpose of overhearing.

As with his diagnosis, Craddock's remedy is drawn from Kierkegaard. Although "overhearing" is not Kierkegaard's word, Craddock uses the term as accurately characterizing important and decisive periods in Kierkegaard's life that he hoped would occur for others. As an example of the power of overhearing, Craddock tells of one such experience that Kierkegaard recalled years afterward:

---

in 1978, he is referring to white mainline Protestant churches in the United States. His observation about the "dullness" of information-oriented sermons excludes other contexts, such as African-American preaching or Pentecostal preaching, where the role of rhetoric, style, delivery, and hearer participation have been and continue to be essential to the sermon.

He was walking through a cemetery late one afternoon when from beyond a hedge he overheard an old man talking to his grandson beside the fresh grave of one who had been son to one and a father to the other. Totally unaware of SK's presence, the grandfather spoke tenderly but forcefully of life, death, and life eternal. The substance of that conversation, not at all addressed to him, was formative for SK's sense of mission, and the manner of his hearing helped determine SK's use of indirect communication. (pp. 105-6)

Craddock notes that if the substance of the old man's conversation with his grandson about eternal life were presented directly to Kierkegaard in the classroom or the sanctuary, it probably would have evoked simply a discussion — or, at most, an argument. By contrast, Craddock describes the influence on Kierkegaard's life of indirect address as "moving," "unforgettable," and "decisive." Not only did Kierkegaard "hear anew" a familiar message of salvation and eternal life that gave him purpose as a writer, it caused him to reflect on the method and style of his writing. Kierkegaard observes: "It also became clear to me that, if I desired to communicate anything on this point, it would first of all be necessary to give my exposition an indirect form."[42]

Craddock attributes Kierkegaard's reflection on his own communication style as leading him to evaluate the merits of indirect address in the pulpit. Kierkegaard observed that the preacher who sends his remarks specifically and directly at the congregation is often not as effective as the one who speaks to them "as though not speaking to them." Craddock summarizes Kierkegaard's style: "A breeze moving over the listeners' heads sometimes quite forcefully stirs them."[43]

To illustrate the use of indirect communication in preaching, Craddock refers to a sermon written by Kierkegaard in *Either/Or.* At the conclusion of the book, Kierkegaard uses the device of presenting a manuscript written by a young pastor of a sermon that has not yet been preached. Whereas the reader is distanced from Kierkegaard's own voice, this technique sets up an occasion for the message to be overheard (*Overhearing,*

42. Søren Kierkegaard, *Concluding Unscientific Postscript,* trans. David Swenson and Walter Lowrie (Princeton, NJ: Princeton University Press, 1941), p. 116, quoted in Craddock, *Overhearing,* p. 106.

43. Kierkegaard, *Journals,* VI, A, p. 115, quoted in Craddock, *Overhearing,* p. 107.

p. 106). Evident from previous sermon excerpts, this technique could easily be identified today as belonging to a "Craddock sermon."

Christian Style: Room and Space

I have shown that essential to Craddock's proposal of distance is the integral relationship between the sermon's message and style. For Craddock, method and style are not value neutral in light of the gospel they communicate. He says that a sermon can be "grossly unchristian" if the "manner" does not match the "matter" of the message (p. 19).

Craddock argues that there is such a thing as a "Christian style," a method of communicating the gospel that is congenial to the nature of the Christian faith. This style is part of the "very fabric of the occasion, of the relationship, of an event, of the truth." Referring to a style that is "fitting" to the Christian message, Craddock observes: "We recognize it when it is present, and we are so aware of its absence that we may have no choice but to stomp out of the room to escape the insult, even if that room be a sanctuary" (p. 20). Throughout *Overhearing the Gospel*, Craddock shows that a primary benefit of distance is "room." His proposal is that distance in preaching preserves not only the integrity of the text but also protects the "dignity" of the hearer. The hearer's defenses are lowered by indirect address. By means of distancing devices in the sermon, the hearer is given room, or space, to consider a message without being lured, pressured, manipulated, or coerced by means of direct confrontation. The result of maintaining distance is free participation in the Christian message.[44]

Craddock, who is especially wary of coercion and manipulation from the pulpit, notes that even with the best intentions, the preacher can coerce the hearer into an emotionally powerful experience that is only "of the moment." This is usually achieved by means of direct address and a confrontational style in the writing of the sermon and its delivery. Distancing devices such as humor and irony provide "oases of momentary disengagement" (Kierkegaard's term) that allow hearers to step back, take stock, get

44. The terms "room," "space," "freedom," "lure," and "coercion" are used by Craddock throughout *Overhearing the Gospel*. For a specific discussion of "room," see p. 97.

their bearings, and breathe. Craddock has said that he did not want the hearer to go home after an emotionally arresting sermon and wonder, "What happened in there?" His hope was that, days later, the hearer would be wondering, "What's happening to me now because of what I heard?"[45]

For Craddock, the benefits of room and space are especially created by an indirect style of delivery that includes the voice, eye contact, and "frame." I will discuss his understanding of distance and sermon delivery later in this chapter.

A New Hearing

Craddock achieves a second benefit of distance — to effect a new hearing of a familiar message — by promoting communication wherein the "familiar becomes strange, and the strange familiar." Craddock identifies English essayist Thomas de Quincey as a master of this technique. Although he quotes him only a few times in his major works, Craddock acknowledges de Quincey as one of the writers who has significantly influenced his own sermon style, especially with respect to techniques that foster distance.[46] In *As One Without Authority*, Craddock quotes the following excerpt from one of de Quincey's essays:

> For, if once a man indulges himself in murder, very soon he comes to think little of robbing; and from robbing he comes next to drinking and Sabbath-breaking, and from that to incivility and procrastination. Once begun upon this downward path, you never know where you are to stop. Many a man has dated his ruin from some murder or other that perhaps he thought little of at the time.[47]

Craddock notes that, if the subject matter were addressed *directly* to the reader, it would sound like a "dull preachment" about life's little things.

---

45. Author interview of Fred Craddock, 1998; see also Craddock, *Overhearing*, p. 97.
46. Author interview of Fred Craddock, 1998.
47. Thomas de Quincey, "On Murder," *De Quincey's Works*, Globe, ed. (New York: Houghton, 1882), 6:573, quoted in Craddock, *As One Without Authority* (Nashville: Abingdon, 1971), p. 150.

With regard to preaching, Craddock says that he learned from de Quincey that, through the use of *indirect* address by means of irony and satire, the hearer can "see in small matters the major stuff of ordinary life."[48]

Another distancing device Craddock often uses in storytelling to effect a new hearing of a familiar message is interrupting what began as a believable story with the fantastic. Challenging the aphorism "you can't teach an old dog new tricks" with the hope of new life in Matthew 13:24-30, Craddock tells the following story in a sermon he preached at Cherry Log Christian Church in rural north Georgia, entitled "What About the Weeds?"

I have a niece in Arizona who cannot stand the thought of [retired greyhound racing dogs] being destroyed, so she goes out and adopts them. She has several of these big old greyhound dogs in her house. She loves them. I was in another home not long ago where they had adopted a racing dog. He was a big, spotted greyhound, and he was lying there in the den. One of the kids in the family, just a toddler, was pulling on its tail, and a little older kid had his head over on that old dog's stomach, using it for a pillow. The dog just seemed so happy. I said to the dog, "Are you still racing?"

"No, no," the dog said, "I don't race anymore."

I said, "Do you miss the glitter and excitement of the track?"

"No," he replied.

"Well, what was the matter? Did you get too old to race?"

"No, I still had some race in me."

"Well, what then? Did you not win?" I asked.

"I won over a million dollars for my owner."

"Well, what was it? Bad treatment?"

"Oh no," the dog said, "they treated us royally when we were racing."

"Did you get crippled?"

"No."

"Then why?" I pressed.

48. Craddock, *As One Without Authority*, p. 149; author interview of Fred Craddock, 1998.

"I quit."

"You quit?"

"Yes," he said, "I quit. I discovered that what I was chasing was not really a rabbit, and I quit."

He looked at me and said, "All that running and running and running and running, and what was I chasing? It wasn't even real."

A whole new life, just like that. That is what I believe.[49]

In this story Craddock creates distance through "willing suspension of disbelief" (a talking dog) and humor (his conversation with that talking dog).[50] Craddock notes that humor may give hearers room at just that awkward or unsettling time in the sermon when lives could be changed in face of new insights. Again drawing on Kierkegaard, he observes that, by seeing the humor in earnestness and the earnestness in humor, the hearer is permitted a decision that, according to Craddock, "is the only human way of demanding a decision" (*Overhearing*, p. 97).

Effecting a new hearing, a device that combines both indirect and direct address, is what Craddock calls the "nod of recognition" and the "shock of recognition." He explains that the nod, "the sense of already knowing and agreeing," precedes the shock, "the sudden realization that I am the one called, the one addressed" (*Preaching*, p. 160). The nod requires distance; the shock requires participation. Craddock observes that this technique, often used in Scripture, is accomplished by indirectly addressing the hearer through a story, immediately followed by direct address.

While the sermon "Doxology" (Rom. 11:33-36), which is printed in *As One Without Authority*, is an example of Craddock's inductive method of preaching, it also serves to illustrate the interplay between indirect and direct address, distance and participation, as he later proposes in *Overhearing the Gospel*. Craddock begins the sermon by telling of his introduction to the "Idea" of doxology. He says: "It was not really a new Idea,

49. Fred B. Craddock, "But What About the Weeds?" *The Cherry Log Sermons* (Louisville: Westminster John Knox, 2001), pp. 29-30.

50. The concept of a "willing suspension of disbelief" is attributed to the English poet Samuel Taylor Coleridge. For a discussion of its function as a distancing technique in theater and literature, see chapter 2 above, "Aesthetic Distance."

but neither was it old. It was just an Idea." He then uses the technique of personification whereby "Doxology" becomes a character. As the sermon proceeds, what at first appears to be a pet later becomes a conversation partner. "Doxology" becomes a companion in Craddock's daily routine of home, errands, hospital visits, vacation, and the seminary classroom. After we have overheard Craddock's journeys with "Doxology," he leads us to his class on Romans 13. In a jarring change of style, Craddock directly addresses the hearer with a question: "Is there ever a time or place when it is inappropriate to say, 'For from him and through him and to him are all things. To him be glory for ever. Amen'"?[51] This question functions as a fulcrum by which the preceding and following story is interpreted. Shifting back to indirect address, he continues the story:

> It was from this class on Romans that I was called to the phone. My oldest brother had just died. Heart attack. When stunned and hurt, get real busy to avoid thought. . . . "I think I packed the clothes we need," the wife said as we threw luggage and our bodies into the car.
>
> All night we drove, across two states, eyes pasted open against the windshield. Conversation was spasmodic, consisting of taking runs asking the same questions over and over. No one pretended to have answers. When we drew near the town and the house, I searched my mind for a word, a first word to the widow. He was my brother, but he was her husband. I was still searching when we pulled into the driveway. She came out to meet us and as I opened the car door, still without that word, she broke the silence:
>
> "I hope you brought Doxology."
>
> Doxology?
>
> No, I had not. I had not even thought of Doxology since the phone call.
>
> But the truth is now clear: if we ever lose our Doxology, we might as well be dead.
>
> "For from him and through him and to him are all things. To him be glory for ever. Amen."[52]

51. Craddock, *As One Without Authority*, pp. 153-68.
52. Craddock, *As One Without Authority*, p. 168.

Whereas the preceding use of direct address in the form of a question gives the hearer something to ponder for the rest of the story, the return to direct address at the sermon's conclusion — "But the truth is now clear: if we ever lose our Doxology we might as well be dead," followed by the ascription of praise — moves the hearer from a "nod" to the "shock" of recognition. Through the device of a personification of an idea, the preacher gives the hearer distance, the room necessary to consider the contexts in which doxology is either appropriate or inappropriate, present or absent. However, by reserving the second use of direct address until the end of the sermon, the preacher "overcomes" the distance (Edward Bullough), leaving the hearer to evaluate the presence and absence of glorifying God in the routine of his or her own life. Through distance and participation, the preacher invites the hearer to *participate feely* in life over death.

Respecting the Hearer: Distance in Delivery

Noteworthy in Craddock's proposal is his emphasis on delivery for achieving the benefits of distance. Expressing that emphasis throughout his three major works on preaching, *As One Without Authority, Overhearing the Gospel*, and *Preaching*, Craddock characterizes *delivery* as the communication of the sermon through the use of the preacher's voice, eyes, and "frame." Together, these components communicate the message of the sermon and create an overall "mood" in the "context," or space, of the preaching event.

A theme that Craddock repeats throughout his works is that the success or failure of delivery is based on its *effect*, its ability to "effect a new hearing," as opposed to its *affect*, whereby the preacher draws attention to her or his own skills and abilities. Craddock notes that a delivery in which the focus is on affect often relies on two uses of a "lure." The first lures the preacher into thinking that personal presence, voice, force of personality, and oral delivery bear the weight of the sermon's effectiveness. According to Craddock, such an emphasis on the preacher's affect does not consider the power of the message. The second lure "draws in," or "catches," the hearer through the affects of delivery. Craddock argues that this lure does not consider the hearer's ability to receive, participate, or reject the message. Such an approach gives little credit or dignity to the hearer. In response to the use of these lures in the sermon, Craddock says: "The Gospel is not bait. The hearer is not a fish."[53] In Craddock's method, style of delivery is like style of writing: there is consideration for the message and the hearer.

As I have suggested earlier, Craddock's warrant for attending to sermon style is the "inseparable relation of the gospel and the forms of its communication." In *As One Without Authority,* Craddock advises that the preacher, with Amos Wilder, should ask, "What modes of discourse are specially congenial to the Gospel?"[54] As if in reply, Craddock proposes in *Overhearing the Gospel* that indirect address is one such mode, a "Christian style" that invites overhearing by means of distance: "Delivery goes a long way in creating what I have called distance, speaking with those present by not speaking to those present."[55] Craddock emphasizes that, once the preacher has decided that a sermon in part or whole would be most appropriately received by "overhearing," then the preacher should consider delivery early in the process of its creation. In the remainder of this section I will discuss Craddock's components of delivery (eye contact, frame, and voice) according to his proposed benefits of distance.

Distance and Eye Contact

Craddock observes that for two decades the preacher and hearer have been conditioned to regard confrontation and direct address as the "only communicative styles with honesty, integrity, and effectiveness" (p. 116). According to him, this domination of the *encounter* and *confrontation* models of communication in culture and the church is responsible for a removal of distance in the sermon through the sole use of direct eye contact. He

---

53. Author interview of Fred Craddock, 1998; see also Craddock, *Overhearing,* pp. 103, 125-33; Craddock, *As One Without Authority,* pp. 31-36, 42-45, 153-56; and Craddock, *Preaching,* pp. 31-33, 168-69, 189-92, 218-22.

54. See Amos Wilder, *The Language of the Gospel* (Cambridge, MA: Harvard University Press, 1970), p. 11, quoted in Craddock, *As One Without Authority,* p. 45.

55. Craddock, *Overhearing the Gospel,* p. 125. Hereafter, page references to this work appear in parentheses in the text.

criticizes speech teachers who train their students to keep eye contact at all times in order to engage the hearer. While recognizing the importance of "eye-to-eye" when the message of Scripture or sermon calls for direct encounter, Craddock proposes the reintroduction of indirect eye contact when the text or sermon calls for indirect address. He argues that just as a wandering eye or distant gaze would give the impression of unimportance to certain messages, it is just as true that certain materials in a sermon are "violated" by direct eye contact with the congregation (p. 117).

According to Craddock, indirect eye contact is especially appropriate to the telling of stories in the sermon:

> A good storyteller seldom looks at anyone. Some whittle, some look into the glowing fireplace, some never stop walking down the lane. . . . They save their eye contact for those occasional didactic turns, when there is a lesson to be planted on the forehead. But these stories are overheard and in that overhearing there may well be encounter and confrontation. (p. 117)

For Craddock, narratives are most effective when they are "overheard," and the distance created through the use of the eyes fosters such an "overhearing."

The benefits of distance in indirect eye contact are twofold. For the hearer, there is "room" to not only participate but also interpret and evaluate the story. Craddock notes that it is difficult to coerce hearers through the use of stories, and for that reason they are usually avoided by preachers who wish to control their listeners by telling them exactly what to think and do. By promoting indirect address as a viable form of eye contact, Craddock is not avoiding encounter and confrontation. Rather, as he clarifies, through the use of indirect eye contact, it is the story that encounters and confronts, not the eyes of the preacher. He proposes that, when the congregation is given room and space through the preacher's eyes, preaching "moments" are "allowed to happen, not made to happen" (p. 117).

The second benefit of distance from indirect eye contact is the protection of the hearer when telling the "Story" of God. Craddock observes: "Without the mediating distance of a narrative, there would be something here too wonderful, too fascinating, too dreadful for our capacity to experience. For the awesome claim of the Story is that the central character is God." Craddock justifies the indirect telling of stories in preaching with the indirect modes of revelation as presented in Scripture. As Moses came down from the mountain with his face veiled, and as Christ was veiled in flesh, so preachers give the report "veiled in a story." According to Craddock, indirect eye contact creates the distance necessary for "overhearing the Story" of God. Because overhearing includes not only participation but also distance, "we are able to endure it."[56]

Regarding the use of eye contact in the telling of stories, Craddock makes clear correlations between indirect eye contact and distance, and between direct eye contact and participation. From a performance-studies perspective, Lilla Heston presents a more nuanced understanding of the function of distance and participation in the performance of narratives. She notes that there are two types of storytellers on opposite ends of a spectrum. On one end is the storyteller who projects the story *outward* to the audience. Those who hear such a storyteller often sit back in their seats and receive the story as presented. From the storyteller's delivery, the story seems to reside in the midst of the gathered hearers. On the opposite end of the spectrum is the storyteller who draws hearers *into* the story. In this case, audience members often sit on the edge of their seats while leaning into the story. From the delivery, the story seems to reside within the teller, and the hearer is invited into the story. Heston makes it clear that the most effective storytellers are those who have the ability to project outward and draw inward — depending on the nature of the story or text.[57]

Heston's observations provide a helpful nuance to Craddock's understanding of distance and its relationship to eye contact. A storyteller either projecting the story outward or drawing hearers into the story would use different forms of indirect eye contact. Yet, in the interplay of projecting outward and drawing inward, there is simultaneously interplay between distance and participation. The implication for preaching is that there are varying degrees of distance and participation in the telling of stories that are not limited to categories of indirect and direct eye contact.

56. Craddock, *Overhearing the Gospel*, 2nd ed. (St. Louis: Chalice Press, 2002), pp. 119-20.

57. Lilla Heston, "Performing the Modern Novel," lecture presented at the School of Speech, Northwestern University, Evanston, Illinois, 1983.

Distance and Body Gesture

Although Craddock mentions "frame" as a component of delivery and therefore a means for the creation of distance in preaching, he does not describe or give an example of how the body can be used for overhearing or indirect address. With regard to the preacher's body, Craddock's proposed benefit of distance as providing space for the dignity and free participation of the hearer could be developed by Charles L. Bartow's work with *kinesthetics* (the movement of the body in and through space) and *proxemics* (the relationship of the body to other bodies and objects in space).

Bartow describes the "space" of the gathered congregation as both personal and corporate. Appropriate distance between the preacher and the congregation can be violated through the gesture of a particular part of the body, such as the arm or hand, or when the whole body becomes a gesture in itself, as when the preacher steps out of the pulpit and chancel into the congregation. Bartow notes that we interpret space in terms of extensions of ourselves. For Bartow (like Craddock), preaching is an "event" involving community, and thus "the extensions of our personal selves in the congregation reach out to the limits of the whole congregation. We are one." Therefore, Bartow urges preachers to take cautious consideration when moving from the pulpit into the congregation as to when it might be right and appropriate and when it might be offensive. When the individual's space and the corporate space of the congregation are violated, hearers may become uncomfortable with the preacher being "elevator close," or they may interpret the inappropriate closeness as aggressive or offensive. In Craddock's terms, the "dignity of the hearer" has been violated by the removal of appropriate distance. Such a violation prevents a "free participation," thereby creating a permanent distance between the hearer and the sermon. The crucial aim of distance, as it was expressed from its inception by Bullough to its baptism by Craddock has been lost: participation.[58]

58. Charles L. Bartow, *The Preaching Moment: A Hands-on Speech Course for Scripture Reading and Preaching*, no. 6, Nonverbal Communication series, PTS Media, Princeton Theological Seminary, 1998, videocassette. For a discussion of distance in the work of Charles L. Bartow, see chapter 5.

Distance and Voice

At the beginning of chapter 2 of his textbook *Preaching*, Craddock presents a basic premise of his homiletic: preaching is an oral/aural event. While recognizing the current influence of the authority of print on preaching, evident by the many sermons that are better read than heard, Craddock holds to his claim that preaching is by its very nature an "acoustical event, having its home in orality not textuality." His emphasis on the oral and acoustical nature of preaching informs his method. He notes that a difficulty when a preacher prepares a written sermon is that he or she is faced with the challenge of "getting it off the page and into the air." Preparation that moves *toward* writing must make the "radically different move" *from* writing. By contrast, Craddock's process moves from hearing to hearing, from speech to speech, from the oral/aural nature of the biblical text to the oral/aural experience of delivering and receiving the sermon. [59]

59. Craddock, *Preaching*, pp. 31-33, 189-93; Craddock, *As One Without Authority*, pp. 154-56. His citations throughout *As One Without Authority* and *Overhearing the Gospel* show that Craddock's understanding of preaching as an oral/aural event and a "Word-event" is directly influenced by the New Hermeneutic theologians Gerhard Ebeling and Ernst Fuchs. Ebeling states: "Ernst Fuchs is right when he says, 'God seeks to speak with us not in writing but by word of mouth.'" What Ebeling calls *Wortgeschehen*, a word-event, Fuchs calls a *Sprachereignis*, a speech-event, thereby placing a stronger emphasis on the spoken nature of Scripture and preaching. Influences on Craddock's proposal of hearing and overhearing is apparent in the New Hermeneutic's "waiting in trusting silence for a word that will be given," "dwelling in the Word," "letting truth happen," and "letting the Word emerge." Influences on Craddock's benefit of distance as room and space for the hearer can be seen in Ebeling's development of Martin Heidegger's later work. Instead of language functioning as a vessel, basket, or room in which the reality of God is *contained*, Ebeling perceives language as *creating room* in the world whereby preaching creates for us meaningful space in existence. See Gerhard Ebeling, *Luther: An Introduction to His Thought* (Philadelphia: Fortress, 1972), p. 30; Gerhard Ebeling, *Word and Faith* (London: SCM Press, 1963), p. 312; David James Randolph, introduction to *On Prayer: Nine Sermons*, by Gerhard Ebeling (Philadelphia: Fortress, 1967), p. ix; Paul Achtemeier, "How Adequate is the New Hermeneutic?" *Theology Today* 23, no. 1 (April 1966): 101; Robert T. Osborn, "A New Hermeneutic?" *Interpretation* 20 (October 1966): 401; Mary Catherine Hilkert, O.P., "Revelation and Proclamation: Shifting Paradigms," in Faculty of the Aquinas Institute of Theology, eds., *In the Company of Preachers* (Collegeville, MN: Liturgical Press), p. 118; Arthur B. Holmes, "Parable as the

According to Craddock, a benefit of distance as created by the preacher's voice is the "room" given in "acoustical space" so that the congregation may freely hear without being lured, overpowered, or coerced. Craddock is opposed to an oral style that, "armed with Holy Writ and the Word of God," "presses in" on the hearer by "pressing down" with the voice. In response to such a direct vocal style, Craddock draws on an analogy expressed by Kierkegaard: "In sawing wood it is important not to press down too hard on the saw; the lighter the pressure exerted by the sawyer, the better the saw operates. If a man were to press down with all his strength, he would no longer be able to saw at all."[60] For Craddock, a style in which the voice is "armed" and "presses in" by "pressing down" becomes an "assault," leaving the hearer no room for lateral movement. Craddock describes this overbearing and imperialistic vocal style as a "verbal massacre." The result is that the hearer who feels verbally imposed on launches a mental counterattack against the preacher or backs away from the sermon altogether (*Preaching*, pp. 63-64, 169). This backing away runs counter to Craddock's proposal of distance as being in play with and leading toward participation.

In Craddock's proposal, the voice is not a weapon but a creator of room whereby the hearer is given the space to experience, reflect, accept, reject, and decide. Because it is an "oral event" that is temporal and ephemeral, Craddock, like Charles Bartow, perceives the sermon to be a "preaching moment." Distance, as achieved through the preacher's restraint in the tone, volume, and intensity of the voice, "allows" for the moment to happen for the hearer instead of "making" it happen. The result is "free participation," as opposed to the hearer's feeling affronted, attacked, coerced, or overwhelmed by the preacher's tone, timbre, intensity, and volume.[61]

Form of the Language of Jesus Which Corresponds to the Incarnation," *Drew Gateway* 48, no. 2 (1977): 15-25.

60. Søren Kierkegaard, *Attack Upon "Christendom,"* trans. Walter Lowrie (Princeton, NJ: Princeton University Press, 1944), p. 181, quoted in Craddock, *Overhearing*, p. 115.

61. Craddock, *Overhearing*, pp. 122-27; Craddock, *Preaching*, pp. 31-32, 220-22. Craddock observes: "The actual preaching of a sermon is a non-repeatable, non-portable event. If a sermon happens to enjoy an afterlife in print, its readers' experience is far different from its hearers' experience" (*Preaching*, p. 32). For a further development of the "preaching moment" as a unique and irreducible oral/aural event, see Charles L. Bartow,

Although Craddock often refers to a singular hearer with respect to distance, it is important to note that the sermon as an oral/aural event becomes the basis for his understanding of the hearing "community." Craddock is clear that the sermon has only one mouth but "many ears" (*Preaching*, p. 31). He says:

> The primary and fundamental nature of word is spoken word. The spoken word is never an isolated event; it takes place where at least two or three are gathered together. It presupposes that which it also creates: community. Spoken words that do otherwise are disruptive and violate the very nature of the church. Paul so informed the speakers-in-tongues at Corinth (1 Cor. 12–14). (*Overhearing*, pp. 43-44)

For Craddock, the sermon does not simply address a community; it proceeds from community and creates community; it proceeds from the church as it builds up the church. Words and the way they are spoken thus can either create or violate the very nature of Christian community. As Richard Eslinger has aptly noted, one of Craddock's most valuable insights for homiletical method is his emphasis on the role of the assembly.[62]

Beginning with the premise that the spoken word is "socially owned," Craddock proposes that the sermon, when preached, is "socially owned" by the collective hearers, having its life and place among a group of participants who are not only influenced by the nature of the occasion but who also bring their "social factors." These factors are not simply brought to the sermon by each individual hearer, but they become "ingredient" to the collective experience of the sermon (*Preaching*, pp. 31-32). Hearers function not only as a community in the preaching event, but they also bring their respective communities to the event. Distance, through the spoken word, provides space for the individual, the gathered community, and the communities brought by the hearers.

The Preaching Moment: A Guide to Sermon Delivery (Dubuque: Kendall/Hunt, 1995), esp. chap. 8, "The Preaching Moment Revisited," pp. 103-12.

62. Richard L. Eslinger, *A New Hearing: Living Options in Homiletic Method* (Nashville: Abingdon, 1987), p. 123.

Summary

In Fred Craddock's method for preaching, distance serves as both an *interpretive tool* and a *stylistic device* for preserving the integrity of the text and protecting the dignity of the hearer. As part of hearers "overhearing" a text, distance prevents facile identifications with biblical characters, easy resolutions to conflict, and familiar interpretations — thereby preserving the text's ability to challenge, offend, and surprise the preacher and hearer. Through the style of indirect address, distance creates *room* and *unfamiliarity* in order that the hearer might freely participate in a new hearing of the gospel. To characterize these stylistic techniques, I have alluded to intentional distancing devices, or alienation effects (Bertolt Brecht), from the works of Søren Kierkegaard and Thomas de Quincey, two writers who, Craddock has claimed, had great influence on his homiletical method and preaching. I have discussed distancing and its manifestations in excerpts from Craddock's sermons, including role-play, point of view, humor, irony, satire, anachronism, and storytelling techniques. In each case, the ability to effect a new hearing of the gospel depends on the relationship between writing style and sermon delivery. In the final section I have illustrated how indirect address creates room for the individual, community, and communities.

I should note that Craddock's call for indirect address as an appropriate sermon style is not a dismissal of direct address. Craddock's proposal for distance in *Overhearing the Gospel* presupposes that the listener already possesses what is to be "drawn out," "evoked," or "stirred up." He clearly says that there are occasions when the listener must first be provided the raw material that is best communicated through direct address (*Overhearing*, p. 84). A reassessment of Craddock's presuppositions and proposal of distance is merited in light of the changes in the hearer in contemporary preaching. I will address this in the next chapter, where I will evaluate charges made by the most vocal critics of distance — the postliberal homileticians.

CHAPTER FOUR

Absorption in the Sermon:
Postliberal Homiletics

In *The Nature of Doctrine: Religion and Theology in a Postliberal Age*, George Lindbeck concludes with this statement: "There is much talk at present about typological, figurative, and narrative theology, but little actual performance. Only in some younger theologians does one see the beginnings of a desire to renew in a posttraditional and postliberal mode the ancient practice of absorbing the universe into the biblical world. May their tribe increase."[1] The "tribe" to which Lindbeck refers has become identified as "narrative" or "postliberal" theologians. Also called the "Yale school," this perspective was instigated predominately by Hans Frei (1922-1988) and shaped by George Lindbeck (b. 1923).

In the early part of Frei's academic career, most graduate schools taught the Bible with little interest in literary approaches to it. Contrary to the methods of biblical interpretation of his time, Frei's response was twofold: first, the Bible should be read with primary attention given to the shape of the biblical narratives instead of the historical context of particular passages; second, passages were best interpreted when beginning with the meaning of the narratives instead of a cultural or philosophical framework into which biblical meanings were made to fit.[2]

Building on Frei's narrative approach to Scripture, Lindbeck developed

1. George A. Lindbeck, *The Nature of Doctrine: Religion and Theology in a Postliberal Age* (Philadelphia: Westminster, 1984), p. 135.

2. William C. Placher, "Being Postliberal: A Response to James Gustafson," *Christian Century*, April 7, 1999, p. 390; William C. Placher, introduction to Hans W. Frei,

his postliberal theological proposal, saying: "The type of theology I have in mind could also be called 'postmodern,' 'postrevisionist,' or 'post-neo-orthodox,' but 'postliberal' seems best because what I have in mind postdates the experiential-expressive approach which is the mark of the liberal method."[3] Lindbeck labels the liberal approach "experiential-expressive" because it treats biblical texts and religious symbols as expressions of fundamental religious experience. This approach interprets both the Bible and doctrine as "noninformative and nondiscursive symbols of inner feelings, attitudes or existential orientations." Beginning with Schleiermacher and continuing through the works of Rudolf Otto, Mircea Eliade, and the liberal tradition, this group claims that the core of religion is the "prereflective experiential depths of self," where the outer features of religion function as "nondiscursive symbols of internal experience."[4] Biblical narratives are perceived and interpreted as expressive and evocative objectifications of an internal religious experience common to all people. For this reason, Lindbeck identifies the experiential-expressive model as a "foundationalist" approach to religious texts, including the Bible. In strong reaction against any kind of foundationalist interpretation of Scripture, Frei and Lindbeck's narrative approach resists any scriptural interpretation by structures, systems, ideology, or experience outside of the biblical narrative itself.

Further developing the work of Frei and Lindbeck for the theory and practice of preaching, Mark Ellingsen and Charles Campbell have made homiletical proposals from their respective postliberal perspectives. In their theory and method, both Ellingsen and Campbell have challenged Fred Craddock's inductive method — with its emphasis on the hearer and its use of "life stories." Since Craddock begins his preaching method with

---

Theology and Narrative: Selected Essays, ed. George Hunsinger and William C. Placher (New York: Oxford University Press, 1993), pp. 5-9.

3. Lindbeck, *Nature of Doctrine*, p. 135. Placher gives a basic definition of "postliberalism" as the "school of theology shaped by Hans Frei, George Lindbeck, and some of their friends and students, also called 'the Yale school,' or 'narrative theology.'" Though Placher admits that these labels are awkward, he notes that Lindbeck himself christened the theological movement as "postliberal," thereby making it difficult for him or his students to object to it. Placher observes that the term has become so broad that it currently is used by "all sorts of people" whom he does not recognize as "members of the tribe" (Placher, "Being Postliberal," p. 390).

4. Lindbeck, *Nature of Doctrine*, pp. 16, 21.

a theological and communicative concern for the hearer, postliberals have categorized his homiletic as experiential-expressive and have thus dismissed it as being self-oriented.

In presenting such a sharp contrast to the role of the hearer in Craddock's method, Ellingsen and Campbell seem to present a distinctively different understanding of the function of distance in the telling and hearing of biblical narratives and life stories. In this chapter I will discuss the role of *distance* and *absorption* in the postliberal homiletical theory and practice of Mark Ellingsen and Charles Campbell. I will then evaluate their proposals according to the "benefits of distance" as previously identified from aesthetics, performance theory, and Fred Craddock's homiletic.

Mark Ellingsen's Homiletic

Retelling the Story

In the beginning of his sermon "We Must be Blind" (John 9:1-41), Mark Ellingsen provides a synopsis of his homiletical method as well as its theoretical warrant. He begins the sermon with what Craddock describes as "direct address" to the hearer:

> What is the matter with you? Why do you never seem to understand what I say? You have ears: Why do you not hear me? Or are you blind? Can you not see what I am doing? You have eyes; why can't you see?
>
> Our Bible lessons for today speak directly to us. It is as if they were written with us in mind. They all make at least some reference to problems of sight and blindness — to the problem that plagues us.

Ellingsen then changes perspectives by voicing a possible response by the hearer:

> Wait a minute, Pastor! You must be kidding. These lessons cannot have much to do with our parish. To be sure, there are a few of us who do not hear as well as we once did or who could use a stronger pair of glasses. Yet none of us is blind or deaf.

Moving again to direct address, Ellingsen answers the hearer's question by providing an emphatic statement of the narrative's relevance:

> Yet to the first question, what does all this talk about being blind (and deaf) have to do with us, I say that it has everything to do with us.

Consistent with his postliberal perspective, Ellingsen does not attempt to make the text relevant to the experience of the hearer other than by saying it is so. This declaration of relevance is based on the authority of the preacher's biblical approach, not on the experience of the hearer. He continues the sermon by informing the hearer how to read the Bible from a postliberal perspective:

> In what ways does blindness (and deafness) have to do with us? I think that to answer that question I should let you all in on a little secret about how to read the Bible. When you read the Bible or think about some of the stories in it, there is a great temptation to think, "Oh, all that is interesting, and it is wonderful to think that God could do this for people long ago; yet it does not have much to do with me." Certainly this is a temptation. However, what we really must do if we want to be open to hear God's Word in scriptures is to be prepared to *locate ourselves in the stories.* We should seek to find ourselves in the biblical accounts, regarding the characters in the Bible to whom God is speaking and interacting as *representing you and me.* We come to learn a little bit about who we are by *identifying ourselves* with these people.

The relevance and meaning of the biblical story is obtained by the self-location of the hearers in the narrative through their identification with its biblical characters.

After establishing his approach to Scripture, Ellingsen concludes the introduction by giving his homiletical aim:

> This way of reading scripture entails identification with the blind man whom Jesus healed. You remember the story . . . this man . . . certainly demonstrated an appropriate gratitude to Jesus, a true faith, did he not? In his faith he teaches us something about ourselves. Like him, we have

all been touched by the good news of Jesus Christ. In a way it has healed us from our blindness, has it not? . . .

To be sure, there is a lot that we can learn about ourselves from the blind man in this morning's story. Perhaps we can learn a lot more than we think. Listen to the rest of the story, and see if you do not gain further insights about who you are.[5]

Ellingsen's goal for preaching is "gaining insights" about who we are from finding ourselves in the biblical story through identification with its characters.

In the beginning of the sermon "We Must be Blind," Ellingsen presents his approach for interpreting biblical texts for preaching as well as the desired appropriate response by the hearer to the text and the sermon. In so doing, he provides a summary of his preaching method as proposed in *The Integrity of the Biblical Narrative: Story in Theology and Proclamation* and embodied in his collection of sermons entitled *Preparation and Manifestation: Sermons for Lent and Easter.*[6]

In the sermon's introduction, Ellingsen credits selections from works by Hans Frei, Erich Auerbach, and George Lindbeck with providing the basis for his "biblical narrative" approach to preaching.[7] This approach perceives Scripture to be a "realistic narrative," much like a novel, in which the hearer is to identify him- or herself with biblical characters within the story. Through this identification, our world is "absorbed" into the biblical world. As the biblical characters encounter God and Jesus Christ, Ellingsen's aim is that we have a similar encounter by entering the biblical story, thereby obtaining self-knowledge and transformation. This approach to biblical interpretation serves not only as the basis of his homi-

5. Mark Ellingsen, *Preparation and Manifestation: Sermons for Lent and Easter* (Lima, OH: C.S.S. Publishing, 1992), pp. 47-49 (italics added).

6. Mark Ellingsen, *The Integrity of Biblical Narrative: Story in Theology and Proclamation* (Minneapolis: Fortress, 1990).

7. See Hans W. Frei, *The Eclipse of Biblical Narrative: A Study of Eighteenth and Nineteenth Century Hermeneutics* (New Haven, CT: Yale University Press, 1974), p. 3; Hans W. Frei, *The Identity of Jesus Christ: The Hermeneutical Bases of Dogmatic Theology* (Philadelphia: Fortress, 1975), p. xv; Lindbeck, *Nature of Doctrine*, pp. 118-19; Erich Auerbach, *Mimesis: The Representation of Reality in Western Literature*, trans. Willard Trask (Princeton, NJ: Princeton University Press, 1953), pp. 13-15.

letical method but also informs his unique definition of proclamation: "a dynamic recital of the biblical stories" where listeners "truly participate" in the story and "allow it to shape their lives."[8]

Although Ellingsen presents many smaller steps in his homiletical method, I will focus on his four main moves in order to evaluate his use of distance: approaching the biblical text as a realistic narrative; interpreting the characters within the text according to their context within the story; making identifications between the hearer and the biblical characters; and "luring" the hearer into the biblical world, whereby the hearer's world is absorbed and transformed.

The Bible as Realistic Narrative

In his preface to *Preparation and Manifestation: Sermons for Lent and Easter,* Ellingsen declares that the basic supposition of the biblical narrative approach is that we should read the Bible neither as the sourcebook for history of the early church, nor as a symbolic expression of religious experience. Instead, the Bible should be read in the same way we read a "piece of great literature." Ellingsen proposes that, if the Bible is to be read as literature, it then follows that the best tools for its interpretation and criticism are those of "literary analysis," for they provide the "most appropriate approach" to interpreting and preaching on biblical texts.[9]

The particular tools of literary analysis that Ellingsen deems most appropriate for biblical interpretation are those from what he terms "early Anglo-American New Criticism." A movement that began in America and England in the 1930s, New Criticism focused on a work of art as an "object in itself," or in the case of literature, "the text alone." According to the New Critics, a work of literature cannot be analyzed or interpreted according to the languages of science, the social sciences, history, or philosophy, for the object has its own language of meaning as "the thing in itself." The New Critics reacted against the mechanistic and positivistic nature of the modern world that reduced meaning to facts, propositions, and systems.

8. Ellingsen, *Integrity of Biblical Narrative,* p. 51.
9. Ellingsen, *Preparation and Manifestation,* p. 10.

They also protested against the Romantic notion that a work of art should be interpreted as a form of self-expression. The early New Critics argued that art should be viewed "objectively" — that is, according to its own language of meaning.[10]

With regard to literary texts, the New Critics exposed the "intentional fallacy" and the "affective fallacy" in methods of interpretation. They perceived the "intentional fallacy" to be the erroneous interpretation of a text according to the intentions of its author. Ellingsen draws parallels between the quest for authorial intent in literary criticism and the source/historical method in biblical criticism, with its attempt to get "behind the text" to the "original meanings" according to an author, redactor, or historical context.[11]

Not only did early New Criticism call into question meaning as found in authorial intent; it also rejected meaning in the text's reception. New Critics exposed the "affective fallacy" as the mistaken attempt to locate the meaning of a text according to its "affect" on the contemporary reader (what would later be labeled "reader-response" criticism). Ellingsen identifies the affective fallacy in contemporary homiletics as the aestheticism of narrative or story preaching. According to Ellingsen, this movement of the last two decades has focused on the experience and feelings of the hearer through its use of "life stories." Using Richard Lischer's essay "The Limits of Story" in support of his argument, he criticizes contemporary narrative preaching for serving the "narcissism of our day" by turning the hearer away from others and inward toward the self.[12]

According to the New Critics, both "intentional" and "affective" approaches of interpretation overshadowed the meaning of the text according to the "text itself." When intentional and affective are used as the two main approaches to biblical interpretation, the result is what Hans Frei calls the "eclipse of the biblical narrative."[13] In order to recover meaning as found in the biblical story itself, Frei proposes a "realistic narrative" approach to Scripture.

10. Jane P. Tompkins, ed., *Reader-Response Criticism: From Formalism to Post-Structuralism* (Baltimore: Johns Hopkins University Press, 1980).

11. Ellingsen, *Integrity of Biblical Narrative*, pp. 9-10.

12. Richard Lischer, "The Limits of Story," *Interpretation* 38, no. 1 (January 1984): 26-39, cited in Ellingsen, *Integrity of Biblical Narrative*, p. 8.

13. Ellingsen, *Integrity of Biblical Narrative*, p. 26.

In *The Identity of Jesus Christ*, Frei succinctly summarizes what it means to read Scripture as "realistic narrative":

> Realistic narrative reading is based on one of the characteristics of the Gospel story, especially its later part, viz., that it is history-like — in its language as well as its depiction of a common public world (no matter whether it is the one we all think we inhabit), in the close interaction of character and incident, and in the non-symbolic quality of the relation between the story and what the story is about. In other words, whether or not these stories report history (either reliably or unreliably), whether or not the Gospels are other things besides realistic stories, what they tell us is a fruit of the stories themselves.

In opposition to any kind of foundational, symbolic, or experiential-expressive interpretation of the Bible, Frei continues:

> We cannot have what [the Gospels] are about (the "subject matter") without the stories themselves. They are history-like precisely because like history-writing and the traditional novel and unlike myths and allegories they literally mean what they say. There is no gap between the representation and what is represented by it.

For Frei, the Gospels as realistic stories "mean what they say," enabling them to portray to the reader their own public world. And the world that they depict is necessary in order for the modern reader to understand the stories, even if it is not the reader's "own real world."[14]

Following in the footsteps of Frei and Lindbeck, Ellingsen proposes that the Bible should be treated in general as a "piece of literature," and in particular as a "realistic novel."[15] Therefore, the Bible should be approached in way similar to how we approach a nineteenth-century novel by Dickens.[16] As a "realistic narrative," the Bible should not be interpreted from its history, as myth or allegory, according to the common experi-

---

14. Frei, *Identity of Jesus Christ*, pp. xiii-xv.

15. Ellingsen, *Integrity of Biblical Narrative*, p. 51. Hereafter, page references to this work appear in parentheses in the text.

16. Placher, introduction to *Theology and Narrative*, p. 8.

ences expressed, particular experiences evoked, or from a framework of preunderstanding. In contrast, Ellingsen says that the Bible should be read in the preparation for preaching as one would a realistic novel, where meaning is contained and disclosed according to the world of the story. He suggests that "the biblical, realistic narrative approach urges us to allow Scripture to interpret itself, that is, to have the text provide its own interpretive framework. The categories and presuppositions one uses in exegesis should always be derived from Scripture" (pp. 28-29).

Ellingsen proposes that reading the Bible as a "realistic narrative" is like reading a realistic novel, "because realistic novels concern themselves with the whole of life, with even its ordinary events." He observes that characters in realistic novels are presented as "real flesh-and-blood people" where "all aspects of their life — their whole world — are presented because their personalities are only developed in relation to that world" (p. 36). By using the tools of New Criticism, Ellingsen's approach entails interpreting Scripture on its own grounds — where characters are analyzed by studying what they do *within the text* (p. 51).

Interpreting Characters within the Text

Ellingsen's next step is the analysis of biblical characters from *within* the text: "In the biblical narrative, Christians seek to know the main characters, God and Jesus Christ. As in any realistic narrative these characters are developed not in isolation, but in the context of the social environment depicted by the biblical narratives" (p. 43). Like characters in a novel, God and Jesus Christ are only revealed through their interactions with the people around them in the story.

This emphasis on the analysis of characters *from within the text* Ellingsen directly attributes to Frei's work with identity and agency in *The Identity of Jesus Christ* and Lindbeck's argument for "intratextuality" in *The Nature of Doctrine*. Describing an "intratextual" method of interpreting Scripture, Lindbeck says:

If the literary character of the story of Jesus, for example, is that of utilizing, as realistic narratives do, the interaction of purpose and circumstance to render the identity description of an agent, then it is Jesus' identity as thus rendered, not his historicity, existential significance, or metaphysical status, which is the literal and theologically controlling meaning of the tale. . . . The believer, so an intratextual approach would maintain, is not told primarily to be conformed to a reconstructed Jesus of history (as Hans Küng maintains), nor to a metaphysical Christ of faith (as in much of the propositionalist tradition), nor to an abba experience of God (as for Schillebeeckx), nor an agapeic way of being in the world (as for David Tracy), but he or she is rather to be conformed to the Jesus Christ depicted in the narrative. An intratextual reading tries to derive the interpretive framework that designates the theologically controlling sense from the literary structure of the text itself.[17]

Whereas Lindbeck and Frei limited the focus of their character analysis to God and Jesus Christ through "ascriptive logic" (the ascribing of the logic of the overall biblical story to Jesus Christ), Ellingsen broadens the focus of intratextual analysis to include other characters within the biblical story. As in Frei's interpretation of Jesus, he does not view such characters as allegorical expressions of ourselves or of a broader human experience. In contrast to the focus of Frei's character analysis, in which Jesus is known only in relationship to others, Ellingsen reverses the process whereby characters in the story are to be analyzed with the same critical tools according to their words, actions, and situation in relationship to Jesus. This reversal is significant as a departure from Frei's original method of interpretation; yet it was necessary for Ellingsen to provide some point of contact between the hearer and the story in his attempt to build a homiletic on a method of literary analysis. Without such a contact, preaching would be limited to a "recital" of the biblical story of Jesus.

Identification and Correspondence with Characters

Once characters have been identified and analyzed according to their context, Ellingsen's next step is the linchpin on which his homiletical

---

17. Lindbeck, *Nature of Doctrine*, p. 120.

method is based: our identification with biblical characters through the correspondence of our lives with theirs. This is the only step that makes Ellingsen's method more than a literary analysis of a biblical text and his overall homiletic more than the reading of the biblical text.

Ellingsen's process of identification and correspondence is primarily based on one of Frei's earlier works, *The Eclipse of Biblical Narrative*. In describing a precritical reading of Scripture, Frei suggests the world rendered in the overarching biblical story is "indeed any present age and reader." Referring to the participation of the precritical reader, he continues: "Not only was it possible for him, it was also his duty to fit himself into that world in which he was in any case a member. He was to see his disposition, his actions and passions, the shape of his own life as well as that of his era's events as figures of that storied world."

According to Frei, "figuration," made sense of the "extra-biblical structure" of one's own particular experience, human experience in general, and concepts drawn from experience. These experiences were all arranged "figurally" into the smaller narratives as well as the "overarching" story of the Bible. Although biblical interpretation became an imperative need, its direction was that of "incorporating extra-biblical thought, experience, and reality into the one real world detailed and made accessible by the biblical story — not the reverse."[18] Frei's realistic narrative approach to Scripture proposed a return to a figurative or typological interpretation of the Bible, in which our world is interpreted according to its incorporation into the biblical world, rather than biblical stories and characters interpreted according to contemporary systems of thought and experience.

Building on Frei's understanding of figuration, George Lindbeck proposes that "postbiblical personages and events" may be interpreted typologically in the same way as Old Testament characters are interpreted. Unlike allegory, which empties characters and events of their own reality, typology constitutes a means of imaginatively incorporating "all being into a Christ-centered world," whether this "being" includes figures from the Old Testament or the contemporary world. As with Frei, Lindbeck notes the "direction" of interpretation:

---

18. Frei, *Eclipse of Biblical Narrative*, p. 3. Frei and Lindbeck use the terms "typology" and "figuration" almost synonymously.

Typology does not make scriptural contents into metaphors for extra-scriptural realities, but the other way around. It does not suggest, as is often said in our day, that believers find their stories in the Bible, but rather that they make the story of the Bible their story. . . . Intratextual theology redescribes reality within the scriptural framework rather than translating Scripture into extrascriptural categories.

Lindbeck's direction of typological interpretation moves from the contemporary world to the text. Nevertheless, Lindbeck cautions that when extrabiblical material is inserted into the biblical universe, there is the danger of it becoming a basic framework of interpretation.[19]

Ellingsen takes Frei's and Lindbeck's "direction" of typological interpretation of Scripture and makes it his aim in preaching: the hearers' identification with biblical characters. In *Doctrine and Word*, he concurs with the effort of postliberal narrative theologians to redefine the theological task as it has been understood since the Enlightenment. He notes that Frei and Lindbeck's narrative approach reverses the process begun in the eighteenth century to interpret Scripture and Christian doctrine in light of our contemporary experience. Contrary to the experiential-expressive model of interpretation, he interprets our contemporary experience in light of the biblical accounts. Ellingsen declares: "We are to appreciate the story-like character of Scripture, and like any good story, Scripture will wrap us up in its tale. It becomes life-orienting when we identify ourselves and our world with its characters and events."[20]

By embracing this typological "direction" of interpretation, Ellingsen rejects allegorical interpretation of texts and especially biblical characters. His interpretation of allegory, as the translation of a text's real — and symbolic — meaning into categories of contemporary human experience, stands in contrast to typological or figural approaches in which human experience is "absorbed" or "redescribed" by realistic narrative.

Ellingsen criticizes two functions of allegory in contemporary preaching. The first is when the preacher uses biblical characters to articulate

19. Lindbeck, *Nature of Doctrine*, pp. 117-18.
20. Mark Ellingsen, *Doctrine and Word: Theology in the Pulpit* (Atlanta: John Knox, 1983), pp. x-xi.

questions raised by their situations in the text. According to Ellingsen, such sermons translate texts into a modern conceptuality in order to answer questions that emerge from human existence. The answers to such questions are then understood as the "real meanings" of the characters and thus the texts. In *The Integrity of Biblical Narrative*, Ellingsen criticizes preaching based on this allegorical interpretation of characters, because when characters and their situations in the story become symbolic expressions of a deeper truth, they are emptied of their *own reality*. What remains are contemporary constructs of the hearer's reality (*Integrity*, pp. 11, 39-44).

Ellingsen describes the second form of allegorical interpretation used in contemporary preaching as the correlation of biblical characters and their situations with the personal sharing of stories by the preacher. According to Ellingsen, this form of allegory serves many preachers who avoid the hard task of exegesis altogether by simply reflecting on what the text means for them. Such an approach produces sermons where characters are used to describe the preacher's own "peculiar experience." Although one might defend such preaching in hope of an identification by the hearer with the particular stories of the preacher, Ellingsen rejects such an approach altogether as being narcissistic self-absorption, which he attributes to the psychologizing consciousness of contemporary culture and a playing on the hearer's desire for entertainment in communication (pp. 7-11, 32).

Whereas Ellingsen rejects an allegorical approach to biblical characters that translates, decodes, or correlates their meaning to our life stories, his preaching method calls for our identification with biblical characters through the use of analogues that exist between some aspect of our contemporary situation and the text's literary context. Ellingsen refers to this use of analogues as "correlation," though he uses the term inconsistently. In his chapter entitled "A Biblical Narrative Approach," he affirms the endeavor to "discern the correlation between the concerns at stake in the biblical text and our present concerns" as a "valid approach for a consideration of any portion of Scripture." In referring to the Gospels, the Old Testament "histories," the narrative portions of the Pentateuch, and the Prophets, he clearly says that "the correlation between our concerns and those of the novel-like portions of Scripture . . . [is] best articulated in a telling of those stories in a way that the listeners are made to feel a part of it" (p. 51). However, when he refers to the process by which a sermon is structured, shaped, and delivered, he rejects any effort to correlate our experiences with those of biblical characters. In the chapter "Designing the Biblical Narrative Sermon," Ellingsen declares: "In the language of much story preaching, *correlation* between the preacher's story and the Gospel's story *does not occur*" (p. 88; italics added).

Rejecting the use of "correlation" in contemporary "story preaching," Ellingsen prefers "correspondence" as the term that best expresses the analogical connection between the hearer and the text in the sermon. In Ellingsen's proposal, "correspondence" with the biblical story is achieved through "analogues" created *from* human experience *to* the characters in the story, not the other way around. Both preacher and hearer are only able to articulate their own stories in light of the characters within the Bible's story (pp. 51, 88).

In this step of Ellingsen's method, identification by the hearer through correspondence with biblical characters, it is important to note that the "concretizing" of the analogues through secular literature or from life stories is optional. "Vignettes" that run parallel to the life issues confronting characters within the text may be used in the sermon, but with limitations: "Vignettes may suggest events in our own lives and contexts or legitimately may function themselves to illustrate the interactions between the characters of the biblical text, provided that the material drawn from these secular sources is employed after the biblical text or its main theme has been articulated." However, Ellingsen specifies that vignettes cannot be used as advocated by the story model of preaching, "as if they had a life of their own and would be sufficient in themselves for the sermon" (p. 72).

In Ellingsen's preaching method, vignettes are optional, for if the original correspondence between characters and hearers is established from the beginning, then "concretizing the analogy" is unnecessary. Such stories from the hearer's life or the life of the community only serve to "clarify" the analogue between the hearer and characters within the biblical story in order to provide the text's contemporary meaning (pp. 89-90).

For Ellingsen, the sole purpose (and limitation) of "vignettes" or "life stories" is to help hearers identify with the characters and their situations in the biblical story. According to him, "there is a variety of images or stories available to preachers for depicting its conceptual meaning for purposes of facilitating the text's existential appropriation by its hearers" (p. 90). The stories are existential only in their "appropriation" of the biblical story, not in an evoked experience that produces meaning. In the sermon they do not function as synecdochic stories that embody the biblical situations today or disclose meaning in their telling, but as illustrations or similes.[21] Like a rhetorical argument, these analogues serve as support or proofs to the hearer of the relevance of the biblical characters' situations to their own lives.

According to Ellingsen's method, identification may take place via the preacher's directly declaring to the congregation that a given text "is really about them." As Ellingsen says in his sermon "We Must Be Blind," "What does all this talk about being blind (and deaf) have to do with us? I say that it has everything to do with us."[22] Throughout the sermon, life stories serve only as clarifications and reminders to the congregation "that they are the characters in the account or the people addressed by it." For Ellingsen, such stories are "optional tools," for once the hearers find themselves in the experience of the biblical account, the stories are no longer necessary (pp. 72, 89-90).

Luring the Hearer into the Biblical World

Ellingsen's final step in sermon construction is a product of the previous one: through the identification and correspondence of our lives with biblical characters, we are "lured," "overcome," and "absorbed" into the biblical world. Here Ellingsen is relying on Frei and Lindbeck's interpretation of Erich Auerbach's description of the power of a biblical narrative that "overcomes the reality of the reader." In *Mimesis*, Auerbach observes:

> The Bible's claim to truth is not only . . . urgent . . . it is tyrannical — it excludes all other claims. The world of the Scripture stories . . . insists

---

21. Regarding the function of life stories in sermons as illustration, simile, and synecdoche, see Thomas G. Long, *The Witness of Preaching* (Louisville: Westminster John Knox, 1989), pp. 156-72.

22. Ellingsen, *Preparation and Manifestation*, p. 47.

that it is the only real world, is destined for autocracy. All other scenes, issues, and ordinances have no right to appear independently of it, and it is promised that all of them, the history of mankind, will be given their due place within [the biblical world's] frame, will be subordinated to it. . . . Far from seeking . . . merely to make us forget our own reality for a few hours, it seeks to overcome our reality: we are to fit our own life into its world, feel ourselves to be elements in its structure of universal history.[23]

Building on Auerbach, Ellingsen claims that in this absorption we encounter God and Jesus Christ, where we — like the biblical characters — are transformed. Noting Auerbach's "tyrannical authority" of the Bible, he says: "When Christians allow Scripture's tyrannical authority to reign in them so that the stories become their own, then the truth of these stories begins to shape their lives." Referring to Karl Barth's "strange new world of the Bible," he continues: "They become participants in its strange new world, the one true reality of God's interactions with the people through Jesus Christ" (*Integrity*, p. 39). Therefore, we are to "fit our own life" into the Bible's world, and feel ourselves to be "elements in its structure of universal history" (p. 43).

According to Ellingsen, the implication for preaching of such a narrative approach is that the world depicted by these stories in a sermon "becomes the real world, the world in which we should really live." He says that "[o]ur preaching should *lure all to become literary figures*, that is, real types of the characters of the biblical world in our own lives" (p. 44; italics added). Ellingsen proposes that, if these strange stories of the Bible are communicated in preaching so that we can recognize ourselves as their main characters, then their reality-transforming authority over the hearer will be manifested to us, and "they will help us to live." Making the Bible relevant to the contemporary world is no longer an issue, for when preaching becomes an act of telling these biblical stories to others, "questions of truth, relevance and modern meaning will take care of themselves because these stories have a way of transforming the lives of those who hear them" (pp. 44, 28).

23. Auerbach, *Mimesis*, pp. 14-15, quoted in Ellingsen, *Integrity of Biblical Narrative*, p. 36.

In the practice of Ellingsen's preaching method, the burden ultimately falls on the preacher to accurately relay biblical stories by following the sermon's narrative form, and to lure the hearer into identification with biblical characters through their vivid portrayal, appropriate analogies, and powerful storytelling delivery.

Evaluation of Ellingsen's Method according to Distance

In presenting Ellingsen's biblical narrative approach to preaching, I have discussed his homiletical method according to its four main moves: approaching the biblical text as a realistic narrative; interpreting the characters within the text according to their context within the story; making identifications between the hearer and the biblical characters; and "luring" the hearer into the biblical world whereby the hearer's world is "absorbed" and transformed. These four overall methodological steps can be evaluated according to the previously established "benefits of distance": the preservation of the integrity of the text and the protection of the role and dignity of the hearer. Drawing on performance theory and Fred Craddock's method of preaching, I will show how distance calls into question Ellingsen's use of early New Criticism, exposes the limitations of life stories for the purpose of character identification, and raises problems regarding community when preaching's aim is to "lure" or "absorb" the hearer into the biblical world.

Distance and New Criticism

The "literary tools" Ellingsen uses in his biblical narrative approach were those of the early New Critics, especially their identification of the intentional fallacy and the affective fallacy in the interpretation of texts. When applied to biblical interpretation, those tools seek the meaning of a text in neither its history, the early church, nor the intent of its author. Nor is it to be found in the response by its readers or hearers. Ellingsen's homiletic is based on a literary theory of interpretation where, as the New Critics claimed, the focus is on the "text alone."

The role of distance in Louise Rosenblatt's "transactional" approach to literature as "exploration" challenges Ellingsen's reliance on early New Criticism.[24] Although sympathetic to the New Critics' concept of the "intentional fallacy," whereby the meanings of texts were freed from "authorial intent," she rejects the "affective fallacy" for its dismissal of what a reader brings to a text and the responses evoked from it.[25] In opposition to early New Criticism, she adamantly argues that meaning is not found in the "text alone." Pertinent to Ellingsen's proposal of reading the Bible as one would a nineteenth-century novel, she proposes that a novel "remains merely inkspots on the paper until a reader transforms them into a set of meaningful symbols. The literary work exists in the live circuit set up between reader and text."[26]

For Rosenblatt, reading a text should be approached as a "performance" in which the reader is both performer and audience. Her insistence on a transactional approach to texts is a means of establishing the active role of both reader and text in the act of reading as a "performing event." Because meaning does not reside in the "text alone," it is neither obtained through "objective" analysis of the text's plot and characters nor experienced through a mystical absorption of the reader into the text. Moreover, the text is not absorbed into the subjective consciousness of the reader. Rosenblatt proposes that meaning be "explored" and "discovered" in "transaction," the interplay of distance and participation between reader

24. As I have discussed in chapters 2 and 3 above, the use of the term "distance" in performance theory and works by Fred Craddock includes the dynamic interplay between distance and participation. Critics, beginning with Edward Bullough and continuing to Fred Craddock, all agree that distance only has its power and effectiveness with respect to the participation of the recipient or hearer. When an artistic work is "overdistanced" (Bullough), or there exists in a sermon "too much distance" (Craddock), engagement is denied, and thus meaning and purpose are lost.

25. Louise Rosenblatt, *Literature as Exploration* (New York: Noble and Noble, 1976); Rosenblatt, *The Reader, the Text, the Poem: The Transactional Theory of the Literary Work* (Carbondale, IL: Southern Illinois University Press, 1978); Rosenblatt, "Act 1, Scene 1: Enter the Reader," *Literature in Performance* 1, no. 2 (1981): 13-23; Rosenblatt, "Reaffirming *Literature as Exploration*," in Edmund J. Farrell and James R. Squire, eds., *Transactions with Literature: A Fifty-Year Perspective* (honoring Louise Rosenblatt) (Urbana, IL: National Council of Teachers of English, 1990).

26. Rosenblatt, *Literature as Exploration* (1976), p. 25.

and text. It is inherent to the nature of the text that it calls for a reader or hearer — and hence a response.

When applied to Ellingsen's literary method of interpretation, Rosenblatt's challenge to early New Criticism accurately reveals the limitations of a homiletic based on the "text alone." By separating the biblical text from the community from which it arose and the community in which it is read today, Ellingsen presents an interpretive theory without a reader and a homiletic without a hearer. The result is a severance of the listener, a permanent distance between text and hearer.

Theory and Method

In his reliance solely on the tools of New Criticism, Ellingsen has few options to overcome the distance between hearer and text. Unlike Louise Rosenblatt's "transactional" approach to literature or Fred Craddock's inductive method, Ellingsen provides no negotiation between distance and participation, no to-and-fro movement between text and hearer. The hearer is either absorbed into the biblical world or remains outside. According to his theory, the duty of the preacher is simply to retell the story.

It would seem to be the case that, for Ellingsen, preaching is only reciting or narrating Scripture. Indeed, homiletician James Kay has made just that charge. Kay quotes Ellingsen: "Preaching is the telling of these biblical stories as realistic narratives." "All claims of the biblical narrative's effectiveness are logically entailed only if the sermon is really a telling of stories." "The sermon must take the form of an actual recitation (*anamnesis*) of the narrative accounts of scripture, a restating of the actual conceptuality used in the biblical treatises and Epistles. . . . Unless the sermon actually takes a narrative form, rather than a mere commentary on that account . . . all the advantages gained by this literary approach to exegesis are forfeited." Kay concludes from these quotes that, once the office of preacher has turned into that of lector, and the biblical narrative form, as *form*, is mistakenly taken to be the exclusive Word of God, "there remains no logical need or basis for preaching."[27]

---

27. Ellingsen, *Integrity of Biblical Narrative*, pp. 45, 46, 92, quoted in James F. Kay's

But, as I have shown, Ellingsen does, in contrast to his stated position (noted by Kay), provide for the role of the hearer in constructing meaning and the role of preaching as more than recitation to encourage listener participation. Ellingsen concedes that, even in their "retelling," narrative portions of Scripture are best articulated when told in a way by which "listeners are made to feel a part of it," for a well-told story "inevitably leads to hearers' participation" (*Integrity*, p. 51).

In his sermon method, Ellingsen provides for listener participation through identification with biblical characters and their situations. Through identification, listeners find themselves in the biblical story and, like those characters, experience the transforming and healing presence of Jesus.

Therefore, Ellingsen's theory is incoherent with his method. He has created a dilemma between the interpretation of biblical texts and preaching. When the focus is on the "text alone," the only method of participation is through absorption by simply telling the story. Yet if listeners are to participate in the story, then method and technique is necessary to draw them in. Ellingsen's "lure" becomes character identification and a "dynamic delivery." Apparently tipping his hat to Fred Craddock, Ellingsen adds that "secular stories" may be used as an "optional application" if the biblical story has been heard before.[28] Because of his dilemma, the listener's story becomes a reluctant accommodation.

Distance and Identification with Biblical Characters

In the final chapter of *The Integrity of Biblical Narrative*, Ellingsen leads the reader through a twelve-step process for sermon preparation that grows out of the interpreter's identification with biblical characters and their situations in the text. The sermon's aim, then, becomes the "analogical"

---

review of Mark Ellingsen, *The Integrity of Biblical Narrative: Story in Theology and Proclamation*, *Princeton Seminary Bulletin* 13, no. 3 (1992): 365-66 (esp. p. 366).

28. Ellingsen briefly addresses sermon delivery at the end of his homiletical method. In under two pages, he encourages the preacher to feel comfortable in the pulpit, use good storytelling techniques, and to practice. For Ellingsen, delivery is "speaker oriented" — with little consideration for its reception (*Integrity of Biblical Narrative*, pp. 93-94).

identification by the hearer with these same characters. If necessary, these analogies can be "concretized" into "optional vignettes" at the beginning of the sermon to help us find ourselves in the story, and later in the sermon to remind us that the biblical story is "our story." Hearers of the sermon are to become "figures" in the shorter narratives, as well as in the overarching story of the Bible. As we recognize the situations of the biblical characters as our own, so their transforming encounters with Jesus Christ will be ours.

Although both Craddock and Ellingsen use sermon techniques for identification with biblical characters, their use of distance in this identification reveals stark differences between the two approaches. In Ellingsen's method, hearers are told through "direct communication" (Craddock's term) where they are to find themselves in the biblical story. Analogies are "concretized" when needed to cement this correspondence between character and hearer. According to Ellingsen's intratextual approach, we are to "fit ourselves" into the narrative; there remains no ambiguity or choice regarding who we are in the biblical story. If such a clear correspondence cannot be made, then the preacher is to choose a different text.

By contrast, Craddock's distancing techniques discourage facile identifications with biblical characters. By jarring the hearer into different perspectives in the biblical story, the preacher questions the hearer's presuppositions of the story. Craddock gives as examples the distancing devices in sermons that are based on well-known stories or parables. As the preacher tries on different perspectives from biblical characters, or creates imaginary characters via role-playing, he or she may reveal surprising meanings in the biblical story — meanings that may resist comfortable interpretations by the hearer.[29] The preacher's use of "indirect communication" gives hearers the space to evaluate where they do or do not fit in the story. The integrity of both the text and the hearers is preserved. Furthermore, unlike in Ellingsen's method, when a one-on-one correspondence is not easily identified, texts need not be discarded.

A second area of difference between Craddock's and Ellingsen's use of distance is apparent in their use of "life stories" (Ellingsen's term) for

---

29. Lutheran Ellingsen admits that Martin Luther preached powerful sermons by taking on the perspectives of imaginary characters, even though the characters did not exist in the biblical stories (Ellingsen, *Integrity of Biblical Narrative*, pp. 49-50).

character identification. Throughout Ellingsen's sermons as he presents them in *Doctrine and Word, The Integrity of Biblical Narrative,* and *Preparation and Manifestation,* runs a consistent thread of the concept that contemporary experiences of sinfulness, disobedience, doubt, pain, or need are analogous to the experiences of characters in the Bible. He usually makes the connection at the beginning of the sermon. For example, in his sermon "What Happens When We Can't Believe It?" (Easter 2, John 20:19-31), Ellingsen sets up a correspondence between doubt as portrayed by Thomas and doubt as experienced by the preacher. After describing Thomas's reaction to the risen Lord, he asks:

> Does this sound familiar? Do such feelings and doubts hit home? They sure do for me. In my own life, you see, I know that the times when I feel the most distant from God are the times when I do not feel good about life or myself. I cannot feel God's love on those occasions, and so it is sort of difficult to believe in him. I cannot see what he is doing in my life, cannot see how he is helping me, and so on those occasions I do not feel like helping him and his church. My prayer life suffers, and I start to feel spiritually dead. Christianity is not very important to me then. I just do not feel like it, and the investment I would need to put in it.[30]

Ellingsen then correlates his experience with that of the hearer:

> "Prove it to me, God! Prove it to me." That is what I am really saying in those moments of apathy and hopelessness. "Make my life good; give me peace, then I will believe and love you, God." Does it sound familiar? Do you hear a little bit of yourself in my confession of sin?
>
> We all sound a lot like "Doubting Thomas" in our Gospel lesson for today.... (p. 105)

After creating an analogy between our response and Thomas's, Ellingsen proceeds to diagnose the problem:

---

30. Ellingsen, "What Happens When We Can't Believe It?" (Easter 2, John 20:19-31), *Preparation and Manifestation,* pp. 104-5. Hereafter, page references to *Preparation and Manifestation* appear in parentheses in the text.

Have you noticed where the problem lies? There is a pattern to our spiritual malaise. The problem is that we are spending too much time, like Thomas . . . being hung up on our feelings. (p. 106)

When he has made a diagnosis of the problem, he provides the solution and cure:

This is what Peter is telling us in our second lesson. This is what Jesus is telling Thomas and us in our Gospel lesson. "People," they are saying, "don't get so hung up on yourselves that you forget God's love. . . . It is not what you feel that counts; it is what God does and says that counts." (p. 107)

In Ellingsen's biblical narrative approach, when Scripture is presented as the solution, doubt will apparently take care of itself.

Ellingsen's published sermons use a problem/solution structure. Although he cautions, in *The Integrity of Biblical Narrative*, that life stories may take on a life of their own and overshadow the biblical story, in his sermons his stories of human situations can be vivid. A limitation of Ellingsen's use of story is that he makes analogies only with the problem and not with the solution. He makes connections between our predicaments and those of biblical characters; but he does not make connections between a transforming encounter with Christ in the biblical story and our encounter with the risen Lord today.

In the conclusion of a sermon for the "Resurrection of our Lord," Ellingsen says: "God has provided (he is still doing) enough to convince us all of the truth of Christianity and of his Son's resurrection — enough to get you excited about your faith. It is merely a matter of living with the Risen Lord, a matter of living with Jesus. He is here every Sunday; he is present in your Bible" (p. 102). According to the function of distance, when the hearer participates in stories and experiences of sin and need, but is distanced, kept at bay, from stories of Christ's presence today, then Christ is risen in the "text alone." Rhetorically, we have only the enthusiastic reassurance by the preacher that Christ is present in the life of today's gathered community.

Absorption and Community

It is with regard to the role of community that Ellingsen's homiletic differs from George Lindbeck's understanding of the function of religion. Ellingsen draws on Lindbeck's *The Nature of Doctrine* to create sermons that "preach the biblical text" so that the "world depicted by these stories becomes the real world, the world in which we should really live." As the text "intends to overcome the reality of readers," so preaching should "lure all" into the biblical world.[31] By combining Lindbeck's narrative theology with the New Critics' proposal of the autonomy of texts, Ellingsen has created a homiletic that has "distanced" the hearer. Although Ellingsen recommends *The Nature of Doctrine* as "the best book written on narrative theology and preaching," it appears that he has appropriated only half of Lindbeck's proposal in that book. By his sole reliance on New Criticism as a sister discipline, Ellingsen myopically focuses on biblical narrative to the exclusion of what Lindbeck calls the "cultural-linguistic" function of story in tradition.

Whereas Ellingsen uses the tools of New Criticism to the exclusion of other methods, Lindbeck combines linguistic theory, sociology, and anthropology to create a "cultural-linguistic," communal theory of religion. From this perspective, religion functions like a language or culture by providing a participatory framework for understanding the world. Like language, religion can shape human experience and generate new experience. According to Lindbeck, religion is not a proposition of an objective reality requiring proof and argument ("knowing that" we believe); nor is it symbolic expressions of experience common to humanity (the experiential-expressive model). For Lindbeck, religion functions as an "idiom" for the "constructing of reality and the living of life."[32] Beneath this "idiom" is the "depth grammar" of story. In order to participate in the faith of a community or a religious tradition, one must first learn its story.

According to Lindbeck's model, preaching would be less concerned

---

31. Lindbeck, *Nature of Doctrine*, p. 188; Ellingsen, *Integrity of Biblical Narrative*, p. 44.

32. Lindbeck, *Nature of Doctrine*, p. 18.

with *knowing that* we believe and more concerned with *knowing how* to participate and live in the community of faith's story. Telling the story means participation in community.

In its disregard for community, Ellingsen's biblical narrative preaching diverges from Lindbeck's cultural-linguistic approach. Ellingsen builds on Lindbeck's claim that listeners are to "make the Bible's story their story," and "it is the text which absorbs the world, rather than the world the text." But these words take on new meaning when put in Lindbeck's cultural-linguistic context. Making the biblical story "our story" is to learn a new language and thus a new way of being *in community.* This is far different from an understanding of preaching as "retelling" the biblical stories, where "truth takes care of itself."[33]

By following the Yale school's earlier use of New Criticism without Frei or Lindbeck's later turn toward linguistics, anthropology, and ecclesial readings, Ellingsen's homiletic has created a nonnegotiable distance between text and community. Preaching becomes a "retelling of the story" without a contemporary community of participants or hearers. It is this turn from the text alone to the function of texts in community that becomes the basis for Charles Campbell's postliberal homiletic.

Charles Campbell's Homiletic

Performing the Scriptures

A more recent contribution to homiletics from a postliberal perspective has been made by Charles L. Campbell in his doctoral dissertation (entitled "Preaching Jesus: Hans Frei's Theology and the Contours of a Postliberal Homiletic"); his book *Preaching Jesus: New Directions for Homiletics in Hans Frei's Postliberal Theology* (a revision of that dissertation); and his article "Performing the Scriptures: Preaching and Jesus' 'Third Way.'"[34] Camp-

33. Ellingsen, *Integrity of Biblical Narrative*, p. 43.
34. Charles Lamar Campbell, "Preaching Jesus: Hans Frei's Theology and the Contours of a Postliberal Homiletic" (PhD diss., Duke University, 1993), hereafter cited as "Preaching Jesus"; *Preaching Jesus: New Directions for Homiletics in Hans Frei's Postliberal Theology* (Grand Rapids: Eerdmans, 1997), hereafter cited as *Preaching Jesus;*

bell's homiletical proposal is based on Frei's later work and its development by Lindbeck.

In this section I will discuss Campbell's homiletic in contrast to that of his fellow postliberal Mark Ellingsen; evaluate Campbell's method and his model of a postliberal sermon according to Craddock's "benefits of distance"; and present his challenges to Craddock's proposal of distance with respect to the role of the hearer in sermon form and style. In light of Campbell's critique, I will reserve a reevaluation of Craddock for the final chapter.

Frei's Turn: From Text to Community

Like Ellingsen, Campbell is critical of the experiential-expressive influence on contemporary homiletics. Both rely on George Lindbeck's claim that the experiential-expressive movement has directly aided in the personalizing of religion in America. Lindbeck is critical of this approach for making religion much more palatable to a society in which the individual's quest for personal meaning is prized over community. He says: "The structures of modernity press individuals to meet God first in the depths of their souls and then, perhaps, if they then find something personally congenial, to become a part of a tradition or join a church."[35]

Building on Lindbeck's category, Campbell criticizes much of contemporary homiletics — and especially narrative homiletics — as being experiential-expressive and based on modern liberal theological assumptions. These assumptions include the turn to the autonomous self as subject, the separation of the self from community, an experience of religion that is subjective compared to the objective methodology of science, the hermeneutic of getting "behind the text" to the prelingual *homo religiosus* of humankind, and structural and foundational methods of interpreting texts and Scripture. According to Campbell, these modern liberal assumptions have serious limitations for the theory and practice of preaching.[36]

Charles Lamar Campbell, "Performing the Scriptures: Preaching and Jesus' 'Third Way,'" *Journal for Preachers* 17, no. 2 (1994): 18-24.

35. Lindbeck, *Nature of Doctrine*, p. 22.

36. Campbell, "Preaching Jesus," p. 2.

As an alternative, Campbell proposes a homiletic that is based on Hans Frei's distinctive approach to biblical narrative and his later move toward a postliberal theology. As I have noted in the discussion of Ellingsen's homiletic above, the early Frei proposed a reading of the Bible as "realistic narrative," in contrast to the historical-critical or structuralist methods of interpretation that "eclipse" the meaning of the biblical story. The tools Frei used were those of the New Critics in order to protect the literal meaning and self-referential nature of the biblical text.

Campbell is sympathetic to Ellingsen's protection of the "integrity" of biblical texts as a motive for using early New Criticism in his "biblical narrative" approach to Scripture and sermon: he concedes that New Criticism takes the text seriously, as opposed to structuralism, which focuses on the "deep structures" that all narratives share in common. But Campbell disagrees with Ellingsen's use of the early New Criticism in placing emphasis on the autonomy of the biblical text. In so doing, Ellingsen has ignored Frei's later turn toward linguistics, anthropology, and community.

Influenced by his colleague George Lindbeck, Frei, in his later work in the 1980s, moved away from the early New Critics' "text alone" understanding to a "cultural-linguistic" understanding of the meaning and function of texts *in community*. Campbell describes Frei's later "communal hermeneutic" as a "far cry from his earlier position, in which he appears to locate 'the meaning' of Scripture solidly in an autonomous text and seems to focus on a formal, analytical method through which disinterested readers may extract that meaning."[37] In a review of a collection of Frei's essays from his earliest to latest work, Campbell notes that Frei's later turn to "the reading community makes the criticism of his earlier formalism virtually irrelevant."[38] In this claim, Campbell has dismissed Ellingsen's homiletical proposal as also being irrelevant.

Campbell describes Frei's cultural-linguistic move as replacing the literary formalism of realistic narrative with the "literal sense" of Scripture:

---

37. Campbell, *Preaching Jesus*, pp. 168-69, 97.
38. Charles Lamar Campbell, review of Frei's *Theology and Narrative: Selected Essays, Modern Theology* 10 (October 1994): 426.

[T]he literal meaning of the text is precisely that meaning which finds the greatest degree of agreement in the use of the text in the religious community. If there is agreement in that use, then take that to be the literal sense. . . . So the first sense of the literal reading stems from the use of the text in the Church.[39]

In "Theology and Interpretation of Narrative," Frei describes the "literal sense" as "the sense of text in its sociolinguistic context — liturgical, pedagogical, polemical, and so on."[40] Frei's understanding of the "literal sense" of Scripture is determined according to "rules of consensus." These rules are determined within a particular community of interpretation, "the Church," where "literal sense" is based on the reading of the stories in the Gospels about Jesus as understood in Christian community.[41] In a post-liberal move, Frei rejects general theories of interpreting Scripture and instead emphasizes the rules for reading Scripture by consensus within the church.

Preaching and Communal Performance

In *Preaching Jesus*, Campbell presents George Schner's critique of Frei's *The Eclipse of Biblical Narrative*:

Essential to the retrieval and refusal which *Eclipse* launches is the recovery of something more than a lost "analytic procedure." Recovering the traditioning of interpretation, the community within which interpretation takes place, and the liturgical and spiritual life forms which embody the vitality of realistic narrative are equally important proce-

---

39. Hans W. Frei, *Types of Christian Theology*, ed. George Hunsinger and William C. Placher (New Haven, CT: Yale University Press, 1992), p. 15, quoted in Campbell, *Preaching Jesus*, p. 87.

40. Hans W. Frei, "Theology and Interpretation of Narrative: Some Hermeneutical Considerations," *Theology and Narrative*, p. 104, quoted in Campbell, *Preaching Jesus*, p. 88.

41. Campbell, review of *Theology and Narrative*, pp. 425-27; Campbell, "Scripture and Community," in *Preaching Jesus*, pp. 83-114.

dures. . . . It would seem that realistic narrative must be somehow independent of liturgical enactment and the community of interpretation.[42]

Campbell agrees with Schner that the distinctive language *and practices* of the Christian community play a central and necessary role in the faithful interpretation of Scripture, and that Frei gave too little attention to these matters in his early work. However, Campbell clarifies that Schner's critique points to key elements emphasized in Frei's later work: the traditioning of interpretation, the community of interpretation, and the "liturgical and life forms that embody the vitality of Scripture." From Frei's later emphasis on the embodiment and enactment of Scripture through liturgy and forms of living, Campbell develops his understanding of Scripture as being "performed" by the community.

According to Campbell, the "cultural-linguistic model" interprets the biblical story by consensus as it is performed *in* the community and *by* the community. This communal performance of Scripture through language, ritual, and action serves as the basis of Campbell's homiletic. He says that within the cultural-linguistic model, "the key to being a Christian is neither a set of cognitive propositional truths nor an individual religious experience. Rather, the key is the language and the practices of the Christian community, which are understood as a set of skills to be learned."[43] For Campbell, the performative nature of Scripture first involves language, and he quotes Frei to that effect: "To learn the language of the Christian community is not to undergo a profound 'experience' of a privileged sort, but to make that language one's own, in faith, hope, and love."[44] Thus, in Campbell's cultural linguistic model, one of the functions of preaching is the teaching and learning of the language of Christian community. Preaching functions as part of the Christian community's "linguistic improvisation" where it not only reflects the language of the church, but also "builds up" the church. Campbell says that, in this "improvisation," the performative, transformative, and participatory character of preaching is

42. George P. Schner, "The Eclipse of Biblical Narrative: Analysis and Critique," *Modern Theology* 8 (April 1992): 170, quoted in Campbell, *Preaching Jesus*, p. 83.

43. Campbell, *Preaching Jesus*, pp. 84, 231.

44. Frei, *Types of Christian Theology*, p. 51, quoted in Campbell, *Preaching Jesus*, p. 231.

retained; nevertheless, from a postliberal perspective, the hearers' participation is understood within a larger communal framework rather than a
private, individual experience.[45]

Whereas Campbell's first emphasis on performance is *language,* his
second emphasis is on *practice.* He describes the "Church's practice of
preaching" as the "interpretive performance of scripture."[46] Campbell
is indebted to the work of Nicholas Lash for the term "performance of
scripture." Like musical scores and scripts for plays, Lash proposes that
the New Testament begins to deliver meaning as it is brought into play
through interpretive performance in the Christian community:

> The fundamental form of the Christian interpretation of scripture is the
> life, activity, and organization of the believing community. Secondly . . .
> Christian practice, as interpretive action, consists in the performance of
> texts which are construed as "rendering," bearing witness to, one whose
> words and deeds, discourse and suffering "rendered" the truth of God
> in human history. The performance of the New Testament enacts the
> conviction that these texts are most appropriately read as the story of
> Jesus, the story of everyone else, and the story of God.

Campbell notes that, for Lash, interpretation does not focus on the meaning of written texts but on the "patterns of human action" by Jesus and his
disciples, and by those who share his "obedience and hope" today. Therefore, the interpretation of Scripture takes place in its performance *by* the
Christian community. This performance is a full-time matter, involving
its enactment as "the social existence of an entire human community."
Lash offers the celebration of the Eucharist as the best illustration of this
performance, for it includes the "life of discipleship which it enacts."[47]

From this performance perspective, Campbell formulates the question, "How does the practice of preaching itself enact an interpretation of
scripture?" In reply, he quotes Richard Lischer:

45. Campbell, *Preaching Jesus,* pp. 231-41.

46. Campbell, "Performing the Scriptures," p. 18.

47. Nicholas Lash, "Performing the Scriptures," in *Theology on the Way to Emmaus* (London, England: SCM Press, 1986), pp. 42-43, quoted in Campbell, "Performing the Scriptures," pp. 18-19.

Just as the liturgy is not a text but an action, so preaching is not a translation of an ancient text but a "performance" of it. And the ultimate "performer," after the preacher has led a sermonic "dress rehearsal" of the story, is the Christian community.[48]

By combining Lischer's analogy between liturgy and preaching with imagery from theater and musical concerts, Campbell provides an answer to his "interpretive question": the sermon functions as a "dress rehearsal" of the distinctive performance of the New Testament by the Christian community. For Campbell, it appears that preaching has become a warm-up for the *real performance*, the actions of the church.

Drawing on Frei, Lindbeck, Lash, and Lischer, Campbell's cultural-linguistic performative homiletic is the preaching of Jesus as enacted by the Christian community. The church's "patterns of action" include rituals of worship and the "active, nonviolent engagement with the 'powers' of the world."[49] From this basis he develops his homiletic according to a set of three criteria as adapted from Frei and Lindbeck: the cultural-linguistic model, an intratextual communal hermeneutic, and the ascriptive logic of the stories in the Gospels. By using these criteria, he criticizes significant figures in narrative homiletics, and in so doing he suggests an alternative.

The Cultural-Linguistic Model

When appropriated by Campbell for preaching, the cultural-linguistic model is a move away from the experience of the individual toward the practice or performance of the gospel in community. Influenced by Lindbeck, Campbell says that the current emphasis on the individual in narrative preaching locates Christian faith in the private sphere, "where American liberal society has wanted to keep it."[50]

---

48. Richard Lischer, *A Theology of Preaching: The Dynamics of the Gospel* (Durham, NC: Labyrinth Press, 1992), p. 91, quoted in Campbell, "Performing the Scriptures," p. 19.

49. Campbell, "Performing the Scriptures," pp. 18-21.

50. Campbell, "Preaching Jesus," p. 220. Hereafter, page references to this essay appear in parentheses in the text.

Campbell is especially critical of what Craddock articulates as "concern for the hearer" in *As One Without Authority, Overhearing the Gospel,* and *Preaching.* He attacks Craddock's inductive method for not beginning with the gospel or theological reflection, but in "good liberal, correlational fashion with the contemporary situation that is somehow self-evident" (p. 233). He charges that Craddock's concern for the "hearer's privacy" through the proposal of "overhearing" Scripture and sermon reinforces private religion at the expense of the public sphere.[51] Campbell also criticizes the New Hermeneutic's influence on Craddock and others such as John Dominic Crossan, for whom, he claims, the "Word-event" is understood as the symbolic expression of human experience (pp. 233-34). According to Campbell, the New Hermeneutic's influence on preaching is responsible for interpretive methods that are foundational and for sermons that are experiential-expressive, focusing on the personal experience of the hearer at the expense of community. From Campbell's cultural-linguistic model, his overall criticism of Craddock is that the hearer's context defines what is possible for preaching (p. 236).

Underlying Campbell's critique of Craddock is the assumption that a focus on the experience of the hearer in preaching is individualistic, excludes community, and precludes social change. As an alternative, Campbell upholds the cultural-linguistic model as providing resources for the contribution of preaching beyond the individual hearer for the "building up" of the church and the formation of the people of God. According to Campbell's proposal, preaching is not absorbed into the personal experience of the listener: preaching, like language, ritual, and performance, is part of the shaping of community.

Intratextual Communal Hermeneutic

Campbell's second criterion is based on Frei's intratextual communal hermeneutic. Developed by Lindbeck and appropriated by Mark Ellingsen in his homiletical method, Campbell's use of intratextual interpretation is

---

51. Campbell, *Preaching Jesus,* pp. 134-35.

where the world of the biblical story presides over the world of the autonomous hearer. According to Campbell, most narrative preaching attempts the opposite.

From this criterion, Campbell is critical of the homiletic of Charles Rice in *Interpretation and Imagination*.[52] Although Campbell gives Rice credit for reflecting an intratextual approach in his sermons, he criticizes Rice's homiletic for beginning with the human condition. Campbell argues that Rice's preaching method begins with the assumption that human experience and contemporary culture are less parochial than the church's Scripture and tradition, and hence should provide the terms within which the gospel is to be made meaningful.[53]

According to Campbell, the biblical story is not made meaningful to human experience; human experience is made meaningful according to the biblical story. Using Lindbeck's terminology, Campbell's understanding of preaching that is intratextual as well as communal is not when the world of the individual "absorbs" the biblical story; rather, it is when the biblical story, as interpreted and enacted in community, "absorbs the world."

Although both Campbell and Ellingsen use an intratextual approach in their homiletics, their approaches differ over the terms "absorption" and "community." In Ellingsen's method, the world of the individual hearer is absorbed into the world of the biblical story through identification with biblical characters. What remains is the biblical world — what Ellingsen calls the "real world." By contrast, Campbell's absorption is not into an autonomous text but into the Gospels as enacted and performed in community. If preaching for Ellingsen is absorption of the hearer into the biblical text, preaching is, for Campbell, the absorption of hearers into a communal performance of text. A significant difference between these two uses of "absorption" is their respective understandings of identification with biblical characters and "character." To clarify this difference, I turn to Campbell's criterion of ascriptive logic.

52. Charles Rice, *Interpretation and Imagination: The Preacher and Contemporary Literature* (Philadelphia: Fortress, 1970), discussed in Campbell, *Preaching Jesus*, pp. 118-20, 128-29, 131-33.
53. Campbell, *Preaching Jesus*, pp. 232-33.

Ascriptive Logic

Campbell's third criterion for preaching is a development of Frei's *ascriptive logic* of the Bible, in which character, plot, and action are "ascribed" to the character of Jesus. Campbell clarifies his use of "ascriptive logic" in preaching by contrasting it to Ellingsen's biblical narrative method. Campbell criticizes Ellingsen as misunderstanding Frei's notion of character, arguing that Ellingsen uses "descriptive logic" to form a homiletic where biblical stories and events are merely described in preaching. In his biblical-narrative approach, Ellingsen proposes that characters in the Bible are as "developed" as any in literature and thus do not need creative additions from the preacher. As fully developed characters, they become the means by which the interpreter and hearer can identify with life situations in the Bible, and hence find themselves in the biblical story. By contrast to Ellingsen's method, Campbell says that many biblical characters are undeveloped, flat, and have little meaning except in their relationship to the larger story and its "subject," Jesus of Nazareth (pp. 258-83). Whereas the linchpin of Ellingsen's method is the identification with biblical characters, Campbell's ascriptive logic emphasizes the relationship of biblical characters and the contemporary hearer of the story of Jesus of Nazareth.

To gain a clearer understanding of Campbell's use of ascriptive logic, we might find it helpful to investigate E. M. Forster's distinction between story and plot. Forster characterizes a story as a "narrative of events in their time-sequence." In comparison, a plot is also a narrative of events with "the emphasis falling on causality."[54] For Campbell, a homiletic based on ascriptive logic does not attribute plot, movement, and thus meaning to individual characters, as proposed by Ellingsen in his emphasis on "identification." Nor does it focus on the form and structure of the plot. This is Campbell's criticism of the attention Fred Craddock and Eugene Lowry give to narrative form and plot as informing the structure and style of the sermon.[55]

54. E. M. Forster, *Handbook to Literature*, ed. C. Hugh Holman (Indianapolis: Bobbs-Merrill Educational Publishing, 1980), p. 356.
55. In addition to Craddock's *As One Without Authority* and *Overhearing the Gospel*, see Eugene L. Lowry, *The Homiletical Plot: The Sermon as Narrative Art Form* (Atlanta:

In Campbell's homiletic, the entire story is "ascribed" to its main character, Jesus of Nazareth. From the character of Jesus, other characters, plots, and actions have their cause and meaning ("Preaching Jesus," pp. 276-83). In Campbell's homiletic, the Christian community's *identification* is with Jesus of Nazareth.

Evaluation of Campbell's Method according to Distance

In summary, Charles Campbell proposes a homiletic based on the communal interpretation and performance of biblical texts that ascribe their meaning from the story's central character, Jesus of Nazareth. From a postliberal perspective, his criteria for the evaluation of homiletical theory and sermon method are as follows. The first is the "cultural-linguistic model." Based on Frei's later turn toward linguistics and anthropology, Campbell's use of this model places the emphasis on the Bible as performed by the Christian community in language, ritual, and action. The second criterion is Campbell's "intratextual communal hermeneutic." Influenced by Lindbeck's understanding of the biblical text's absorbing the world, Campbell uses intratextuality to reject the experiential-expressive movement's emphasis on the personal experience of the hearer in contemporary narrative homiletics. According to Campbell, Craddock's inductive method and proposal for overhearing are experiential-expressive in their concern for the experience of the hearer. The third criterion is ascriptive logic, in which the character, plot, and action of the biblical story — as well as preaching — ascribe their meaning according to their main character, Jesus of Nazareth.

In the remainder of this chapter, I will evaluate Campbell's postliberal homiletic and its criteria according to Fred Craddock's proposal of distance. For Craddock, distance functions as a hermeneutical tool and a stylistic device in sermon construction and delivery. As I did with Ellingsen, I will begin with a discussion of Campbell's sermon method and then move to his proposed sermon model of postliberal preaching.

John Knox, 1989); see also Lowry, *How to Preach a Parable: Designs for Narrative Sermons* (Nashville: Abingdon, 1989).

Sermon Form and Method

In Campbell's 257-page book *Preaching Jesus*, he dedicates approximately ten pages to sermon form, and he pays even less attention to sermon method and construction. This lack of emphasis is not an oversight, but is intentionally based on Frei's ascriptive logic. Campbell says that the issue at stake in sermon form can be interpreted within the framework of narrative itself:

> While contemporary narrative homiletics has been concerned with formal matters of plot, Frei's work shifts the focus to the particular matter of character. This simple shift of focus has significant implications. Whereas for homileticians the narrative shape of the Gospels has led to a focus on plot and sermon form, for Frei the narrative shape leads to an emphasis on character and Christology. According to Frei, Christians are interested in narrative only because Jesus is what he does and undergoes, not because of anything magical about narrative form per se.[56]

Following Frei's "ascriptive logic," Campbell interprets an emphasis on the form of the sermon — in what he calls "narrative homiletics" — as being based on the formal matters of plot instead of character. He criticizes such proposals for ignoring the identity of God or Jesus as crucial for the particular narratives of the Christian community. In a footnote, Campbell does admit that Craddock mentions in *Overhearing the Gospel* that the central character in the biblical narrative is God; however, Campbell would reject Craddock's proposal of distance as "fitting" for a "Christian style" as an emphasis of form and method at the expense of the character of Jesus.[57]

Campbell also criticizes Craddock's use of parables as a model for sermon form and style. For Craddock, the parable form and style indirectly addresses the hearer in order to effect a new hearing through overhearing. The sermon can be overheard in the same way, and thereby the gospel can be "heard anew." Campbell quotes Craddock from *Overhearing the Gospel*:

56. Campbell, *Preaching Jesus*, p. 171. Hereafter, page references to this book appear in parentheses in the text.

57. Craddock, *Overhearing the Gospel*, p. 140, referred to in a footnote by Campbell in *Preaching Jesus*, p. 171.

"The parable is the example par excellence of a piece of literature that is not designed to convey information but by its very form arrests attention, draws the listener into personal involvement, and leaves the final resolution of the issue to the hearer's own judgment." Campbell summarizes Craddock's method as beginning with "common human experience" that moves to an "open-ended, experiential point," which "forces the individual hearer to decide in his or her existential situation" (pp. 174-75).[58]

It should be noted that Campbell's summary bears closer resemblance to Bultmann than to Craddock. Leaving the final resolution up to the "hearer's own judgment" is not forcing the hearer to a "decision." A forced decision contradicts Craddock's proposal of overhearing, in which the "benefits of distance" are the space for free participation. Even so, Campbell would disregard these benefits of distance for the hearer as being "experiential."

Campbell states that the ascriptive logic of the Gospel narratives suggests "helpful theological guidelines for preparing and analyzing sermons, including narrative sermons, at a level much deeper and more profound than that of sermon form" (p. 201). Returning to Craddock's terms for the separation between method and message, Campbell's statement here reflects the severing of the "how" from the "what" in the preaching of the gospel. This demotion of form and style to the "less profound" endeavors of preaching is what differentiates Campbell's homiletical theory from Craddock's homiletical theory and method. Distance is of no concern when form, not to mention style, is given little consideration with respect to sermon content. Even so, Campbell notes that Frei's turn from parable to gospel and from plot to character has "significant implications for preaching" and "some interesting consequences" for sermon form (p. 201).

In the segment of *Preaching Jesus* entitled "The Story of Jesus and Sermon Form," Campbell makes it clear that "Frei had no real stock in narrative form or stories per se," and for this reason distanced himself from forms of "narrative theology" (p. 202). Campbell clarifies that Frei's sermons did not take on narrative forms; rather, Frei preferred "colonial Puritan sermons" comprised of exegesis and application. By contrast to sermons that "inductively" move from human experience to the text,

58. Quoting Craddock, *Overhearing the Gospel*, p. 77.

Campbell describes Frei's sermons as moving from the biblical text to the contemporary situation. In Campbell's book *Preaching Jesus*, this appears to be the only attention to sermon form given in a positive light. Yet, in this method there remains for the preacher and the hearer an unbridged distance between exegesis and application.

What Campbell overlooked in his description of "colonial Puritan sermons" is the step between exegesis and application. As I have shown in my discussion of "Puritan Plain Style" preaching (chapter 3 above), the move from "giving the sense and understanding of the text according to the scripture itself," to the application of these "doctrines to the life and manners of the congregation," was made through the "collection" of a "few and profitable points of doctrine." The distance between exegesis and application was bridged through proposition. According to William Perkins (1558-1602), in his homiletical handbook *The Art of Prophesying*, application was optional, depending on if the preacher "has the gift."[59] Although Campbell emphasizes the performative nature of preaching in the community, the only homiletical method he provides is the propositional form of presenting points of doctrine in which application to the congregation is an optional addition. According to Craddock's proposal, preaching that is performative is not limited to proposition but is also evocative.

Although Campbell claims that Frei's "Theological Reflections" and *The Identity of Jesus Christ* suggest the "complexity of the relationship" between the story of Jesus and its homiletical appropriation, Campbell provides little discussion about what that relationship might be with regard to sermon construction or form. It appears that any form or style — even narrative — can be used, as long as there is no theoretical or theological rationale to warrant its use. He would dismiss such a warrant as "experiential-expressive," "foundational," or "liberal." As long as the sermon focuses on the logic of the narratives in the Gospels, it appears that any form will do. This absence of form not only violates Craddock's theological concern for the hearer; it provides the preacher little help in

59. See Horton Davies, *Studies of the Church in History* (Allison Park, PA: Pickwick Publications, 1983), pp. 104-7; William Perkins, *The Art of Prophesying with The Calling of Ministry* (Edinburgh: Banner of Truth Trust, 1996; first published 1607); Joseph A. Pipa Jr., "William Perkins and the Development of Puritan Preaching" (PhD diss., Westminster Theological Seminary, 1985), text-fiche.

performing the logic of the gospel through the construction and delivery of the sermon.

In the section of *Preaching Jesus* that is dedicated to sermon form, Campbell opens the discussion by quoting James F. Kay's statement regarding the consequences of Frei's work for homiletics: "[T]here really remains no logical need for preaching in any sense other than narrative recitation."[60] Campbell proceeds to refute Kay's assertion that Frei's work constrains the preacher "to do nothing more than simply recite verbatim the biblical narratives" by suggesting "the rich and complex ways in which the story of Jesus and sermons may be related" (pp. 201-2, 211).

In developing Frei's thought, Campbell attempts the move from text to sermon through Richard Hays's examination of Paul's use of "discursive speech" and allusion with respect to the "narrative substructure" of Galatians. Thus, like Paul, preachers need to explore discursive language that moves neither deductively from the abstract nor inductively from human experience. As in Paul's letters, sermons are to be "continuous and organic" as they operate in the "narrative logic" of the story of Jesus. Yet the fruit of this attempt regarding sermon form is merely this: "The relationship between narrative text and sermon form is more complicated than many contemporary narrative homileticians have suggested" (p. 211).

Campbell concludes his discussion on sermon form by saying, "Far from constricting the relationship between biblical narrative and sermon form, Frei's work suggests more complex and expansive ways of exploring this relationship" (p. 211). Although Campbell does not provide a clear method in the movement between text and sermon form, he does offer a model.

Sermon Model

In *Preaching Jesus*, Campbell offers, as a postliberal model, Walter Brueggemann's sermon entitled "Pain Turned to Newness," based on Mark

---

60. James F. Kay, "Theological Table Talk: Myth or Narrative?" *Theology Today* 48 (October 1991): 326-32, quoted in Campbell, *Preaching Jesus*, p. 201.

5:24b-34.[61] After criticizing a sermon by Wayne Bradley Robinson for its "stereotyped plot" that moves from issue to resolution, Campbell praises Brueggemann's sermon for simply following the biblical story through its "dramatic reenactment" for the hearers. Unlike the experiential-expressive model, Campbell observes that the sermon "begins with the story, not with human experience." Campbell holds up Brueggemann's sermon as "one possible form" that embodies Frei's work, in which "text, exposition, and congenial application are inseparable and dramatically woven together" (p. 197).

In my discussion of the form and style of "Pain Turned to Newness," I will put into dialogue Campbell's cultural-linguistic criteria of intratextual hermeneutic and ascriptive logic with Craddock's function of distance and its benefits for the biblical text and hearer.

On the printed page, the sermon is divided into an introduction and four scenes. Campbell describes the introduction as highlighting the "intrusive, inconvenient character" of the woman with the flow of blood, whose story interrupts that of the "powerful, influential leader of the synagogue." Before reenacting the story, Brueggemann suggests the woman's story may be ours — "Listen to her story as a tale about your own life and our life" — an invitation that meets Campbell's criterion of an intratextual hermeneutic. Campbell observes that hearers are not invited to find their stories in the biblical story as is often encouraged in narrative preaching. Instead, Brueggemann "redescribes" their stories according to the biblical story. Using the words of Lindbeck, he says that Brueggemann's sermon "does not suggest, as is often said in our day, that believers find their stories in the Bible, but rather they make the story of the Bible their story."[62]

In his discussion of the four scenes of the sermon, Campbell uses the criterion of ascriptive logic as supported by typology to evaluate Brueggemann's portrayal of biblical characters. Campbell begins with the woman with the issue of blood. Based on Frei's study of typology in *The Eclipse of Biblical Narrative*, he characterizes her as a "type" of a person in pain, yet without losing her "distinctively contingent or random individuality"

61. Walter Brueggemann, "Pain Turned to Newness," preached at Columbia Theological Seminary, May 9, 1992, quoted in Campbell, *Preaching Jesus*, pp. 259-64.

62. George Lindbeck, *Nature of Doctrine*, p. 118, quoted in Campbell, *Preaching Jesus*, p. 197.

(p. 198). Campbell then discusses the "typology" of Jesus in the sermon. Though Jesus is not mentioned directly in the first scene of the story, his presence is foreshadowed as an "embodiment," or type, of power. When Jesus comes into the scene, his "unique and unsubstitutable identity" begins to become apparent. As he is being touched by and at the same time is healing someone, the "strange and unique conjunction of power and powerlessness in Jesus' person" becomes clear. By the time Jesus speaks to the woman, in the third scene, Campbell claims that Jesus has fully emerged as a "unique, unsubstitutable person," who, in the words of Brueggemann, "acts out and models a new way of power towards pain" (pp. 198-99).

Though Campbell rejects Craddock's proposal of overhearing and distance for absorbing the biblical story into the private experience of the individual, Brueggemann uses distancing devices throughout the sermon that Campbell admires. In fact, it is surprising how well the sermon embodies many aspects of Craddock's proposal. Although Campbell shows little interest in sermon form and style, I propose that the power and "effectiveness" of the sermon's message is directly dependent on its stylistic devices of communication. From the careful construction of the sermon, Brueggemann uses such devices and thus reveals an intentional consideration of the hearer. Some of the devices of distance are the following:

Brueggemann retells the story in Mark via the form and style of dramatic reenactment. Although his introduction begins by describing how the woman's story interrupts a larger story, Brueggemann neither proposes the story's point or meaning, nor does he present a thesis to be supported by the rest of the sermon. As Brueggemann proceeds with the reenactment, his style is dramatic, narrative, and thus inductive. In Craddock's terms, Brueggemann "effects" an overhearing of the sermon and biblical story through storytelling in order for the gospel to be heard anew.

Before proceeding to the narrative, Brueggemann *invites* us to participate in the woman's story, because "her story might turn out to be our story as well." According to Craddock's benefits of distance, such an invitation provides hearers the space for consideration, evaluation, and free participation. In this request, the hearer is both individual and corporate. Brueggemann says: "Listen to her story as a tale about your own life and our life" (pp. 259-60). However, unlike Ellingsen's sermon "We Must Be

Blind," Brueggemann is not forcing a one-on-one correspondence between the hearer and a biblical character.

In the sermon's final scene, we are given the opportunity to recognize ourselves in many characters in the story, even seeing how we share human characteristics with Jesus. As illustrated in sermons by Craddock, identification with multiple characters creates a distance that protects both the biblical text and the hearer. By preventing a facile identification with a particular biblical character, the preacher protects the conflict and challenge of the text from comfortable interpretations. By giving the hearer the space to identify with many characters, the preacher protects the hearer from coercion by the preacher.

In his proposal for distance, Craddock encourages the preacher's indirect address of the hearer through storytelling and role-playing. As we have previously discussed, Craddock's call for indirect address as an appropriate sermon style is not a dismissal of direct address. As excerpts from his sermons have shown, Craddock often uses a combination of the two, interplaying the distance of overhearing with the full participation of being directly addressed by the gospel. Again, Brueggemann's sermon serves as a model for Craddock as well as for Campbell. The three scenes of storytelling are framed by the direct address of the introduction, "Listen to her story as a tale about your own life and our life," and the last line of the sermon, "Go in peace, be healed of your disease, by your faith be whole" (pp. 259-60, 264).[63] In Craddock's terms, what was addressed to the woman is now directly addressed to us. What was overheard is now hearing anew.

Although there are surprising similarities between the style of "Pain Turned to Newness" and sermons by Craddock, there remains a significant difference in regard to distance, absorption, and the contemporary hearer. Scene Four begins:

> You recognize, do you not, your own place in this story. We are all hemorrhaging women, with life bleeding out of us, tired of being abused,

63. I should note that, though Brueggemann's use of indirect and direct address is similar to Craddock's style, the large amount of direct address in the sermon's conclusion and the strong use of "you" would probably be too heavy-handed for Craddock's approach.

with exhausted resources, scarcely able one more time to reach out for a touch. We are all of us part of the busy disciples, too busy with numbers to notice, too important and preoccupied. We are not Jesus, but we do as baptized folk share in his power and in his capacity to heal, to let ourselves be touched so that some of our God-given power can flow to the lives of other bleeding outsiders. We are also the by-standing folk who watch in astonishment. We watch because this hurting woman and this caring agent of God, this odd text, provide a new shape for social relations. It is a shape that generates new possibility, new changes for communion, and new patterns of social power. (Quoted in *Preaching Jesus*, p. 264)

Although Campbell describes the sermon's final scene as carrying the story into the time of the contemporary hearer, I contend that the opposite is true. According to ascriptive logic, Campbell is clear that we are invited to become characters *in the story of Jesus*. According to a "communal intratextual hermeneutic," the story "redescribes the world and calls the hearers to discipleship" (p. 199). Similar to Mark Ellingsen's sermon "We Must be Blind," Brueggemann's "Pain Turned to Newness" uses identification (with the characters) for absorption into the story. Where the two differ is that Ellingsen uses a one-on-one identification between an individual hearer and an individual character, whereas Brueggemann's identification is typological and corporate. As Brueggemann says, "We are all hemorrhaging women," and, like Jesus, we are agents of "God-given power for healing" (quoted in *Preaching Jesus*, p. 264).

By contrast to Craddock's concern for the hearer, both Bruggemann and Ellingsen end their sermons in what can be characterized as a postliberal style. Contemporary hearers are told that the biblical story is relevant to their lives, but there is no embodiment of that relevance for today. Although Brueggemann proclaims that we are the "caring agent of God," there are no stories and no performances of "a new shape of social relations" and "new patterns of social power" in today's world. A significant limitation of a postliberal sermon is that the gospel story appears to end in the Bible. We are to encounter Jesus Christ in the biblical world; Jesus Christ does not encounter us in ours. What remains for the hearer is the biblical story with only a claim of relevance by the preacher.

Craddock's emphasis on sermon form and style is based on a theological concern for the communication of the gospel in the lives of contemporary hearers. According to Craddock's proposal, Campbell's separation of sermon form and style from content is a separation of the contemporary hearer from the gospel message. Although Campbell's emphasis on preaching as communal performance shows promise for discipleship and the building up of the church, his disregard for form and style reveals a neglect of the performative nature of the sermon and its transformative potential for hearer participation.

Absorption Reconsidered

The Dilemma

In this chapter I have argued that both Ellingsen and Campbell, from their respective postliberal perspectives, wrote homiletical proposals in which their theory contradicts their methods and models for sermon form and style. By attempting a homiletic based on Frei's approach to Scripture, Campbell and Ellingsen create a dilemma between a hermeneutic of absorption and a sermon method that involves the hearers' participation. Such a method requires attention to sermon form, style, and delivery. Ellingsen attempts to overcome this dilemma by way of character identification, but, as I have argued, his method is incoherent with his theory of the "text alone." Campbell attempts to overcome the dilemma by way of the cultural-linguistic approach to Scripture that Frei presented in his later works.

A significant influence on Frei's "turn" toward culture was anthropologist Clifford Geertz. Frei takes Geertz's statement that "culture consists of socially established structures of meaning," and he applies it to the church:

> I'm suggesting that the Church is very much like that — a culture, not only of course for the observer but also for the agent, the adherent, who would understand it. There is a sacred text — a typical element in a religious system — and there are informal rules and conventions governing how the sign system works in regard to sacred scripture. The kind of

theology that I like best is the kind that is closer to this outlook rather than to philosophy, or to historiography.[64]

In Frei's cultural-linguistic turn, the meaning of scriptural texts is not in what they say but in how they are used and "what they do" in the life of the community.[65] Therefore, Frei turns to the anthropologist instead of the philosopher, historiographer, or literary critic, as best qualified to interpret the use and performance of texts in community.

Nevertheless, this turn is incomplete. Mark Lewis Taylor rightly notes that, though Frei began to draw on the work of anthropologist Clifford Geertz to create a cultural-linguistic approach to Scripture, Frei shows none of Geertz's "thick description" for the interpretation of communities. Regarding Frei's proposal, Taylor says: "[I]n the end the 'cultural' drops out, leaving only 'texts.'"[66]

Geertz proposes that one of the tools for "thick description" is the use of distance for the study and interpretation of communities and cultures. Using the terms of psychoanalyst Heinz Kohut, Geertz distinguishes between "experience-near" and "experience-distant" concepts. He describes an "experience-near" concept as one that an individual might "naturally and effortlessly use to define what he or his community feel, think, imagine . . . and which he would readily understand when similarly applied by others." He then describes an "experience-distant" concept as one that "various types of specialists — an analyst, an experimenter, an ethnographer, even a priest or an ideologist — use to forward their scientific, philosophical, or practical aims."[67] Ironically,

---

64. Clifford Geertz, *The Interpretation of Cultures* (New York: Basic Books, 1973), pp. 12-13, quoted and commented on in Frei, *Types of Christian Theology*, p. 13; see also William C. Placher, introduction to Frei, *Theology and Narrative*, pp. 17-18.

65. "What they do" is from Jean-François Lyotard's statement that narratives "define what has the right to be said and done in the culture in question, and since they are themselves a part of that culture, they are legitimated by the simple fact that they do what they do." See *The Postmodern Condition: A Report on Knowledge*, trans. Geoff Bennington and Brian Massumi (Minneapolis: University of Minnesota Press, 1984), p. xxiii, quoted in Placher, introduction to Frei, *Theology and Narrative*, pp. 18-19.

66. Author interview of Mark Lewis Taylor, Princeton Theological Seminary, Princeton, New Jersey, 2003.

67. Clifford Geertz, "From a Native's Point of View," in Paul Rabinow and Wil-

the importance Geertz places on distance in anthropology is quite similar to Craddock's function of distance in preaching. Geertz's understanding of distance for reflection, in order to place experience in a broader context of meaning, is congruent with Craddock's critical distance between hearer and sermon.

As is evident from Geertz's study of distance, a cultural approach takes seriously the *experiences* of members of a community, as well as texts and rituals. When applied to preaching, a "thick description" would take into consideration the experience of hearing as well as biblical texts and their enactment in community. This interpretation of the hearers, including what effects a hearing, Craddock identifies as the "sermon in context." Yet such an emphasis on the hearer's experience and context has been challenged and rejected by Campbell as being experiental-expressivist. Even with Campbell's cultural-linguistic turn, the dilemma among text, sermon, and hearer remains.

Reading and Performance

The homiletical dilemma of both Ellingsen and Campbell has its source in their proposal of the "absorption" of hearers into the "real world" of the story of the Bible. This concept of absorption is based on Frei's and Lindbeck's reading of Erich Auerbach's *Mimesis: The Representation of Reality in Western Culture.* Campbell argues that although Frei relies on Auerbach to create his interpretive approach to the Bible as "realistic narrative," Auerbach's views are also consistent with Frei's turn toward the cultural-linguistic model. Even within this cultural-linguistic turn, absorption of the hearer's world into the "real world" of the Bible continues to be at the basis of the postliberal approach, what Lindbeck calls the "ancient practice of absorbing the universe into the biblical world."[68]

In their use of "absorption," both Frei and Lindbeck draw on Erich Auerbach's discussion of the works of Homer and the Old Testament. While

---

liam M. Sullivan, eds., *Interpretive Social Science: A Reader* (Berkeley: University of California Press, 1979), pp. 226-27.

68. Lindbeck, *Nature of Doctrine*, p. 135.

we can note the differences between the two styles of the Homeric epic and the Old Testament narratives, an analysis of Auerbach's discussion reveals what they share in common is the "real world rendered," into which the reader is "lured." Auerbach says: "The oft-repeated reproach that Homer is a liar takes nothing from his effectiveness, he does not need to base his story on historical reality, his reality is powerful enough in itself; it ensnares us, weaving its web around us, and that suffices him. And this 'real' world into which we are lured, exists for itself, contains nothing but itself."[69] Thus do the works of Homer "bewitch" the readers and "ingratiate" themselves until the readers live with them "in the reality of their lives" (p. 13).

While comparing the Old Testament to the works of Homer, Auerbach notes that the Old Testament stories do not "bewitch the senses," but their religious intent involves an "absolute claim to historical truth." Auerbach proposes that such a truth claim is far more urgent than Homer's, and he characterizes it as "tyrannical." He says that the Bible "insists that it is the only real world, is destined for autocracy. All other scenes, issues, and ordinances have no right to appear independently of it, and it is promised that all of them, the history of all mankind, will be given their due place within its frame, will be subordinated to it" (p. 15). Thus the "tyranny" of the Bible is that it absorbs not only the reader, but, to use Lindbeck's phrase, it absorbs "the universe into the biblical world."

In his comparison of the Homeric and Old Testament styles, Auerbach declares:

> Since we are using the two styles, the Homeric and the Old Testament, as starting points, we have taken them as finished products, as they appear in the texts; we have disregarded everything that pertains to their origins, and thus have left untouched the question whether their peculiarities were theirs from the beginning or are to be referred wholly or in part to foreign influences. Within the limits of our purpose, a consideration of this question is not necessary; for it is in their full development, which they reached in early times, that the two styles exercised their

---

69. Auerbach, *Mimesis*, p. 13. Hereafter, page references to this work appear in parentheses in the text.

determining influence on the representation of reality in European literature. (p. 23)

Auerbach's proposal of absorption is based on "reading" the "finished product" of the Old Testament, and especially Homer. By disregarding the formation of these works, he has ignored their origin in oral performance and their tradition as orally performed.

Auerbach's understanding of absorption, or "lure," as based on the reading of a completed work by Homer can be challenged by the work of Alfred B. Lord in *The Singer of Tales*. Lord proposes that, for Homer, like the contemporary oral poet, the moment of composition is the *performance*. An oral poem is not composed *for* but *in* performance through the audience's response. This mutual response between both performer and audience includes interplay between distance and participation. The story is always altered and created according to the hearers who participate. Contrary to Auerbach's *reading* of Homer, there is no absorption into a world of the text. The text is created through the participation of the hearers *in the performance*.[70]

---

70. Alfred B. Lord, in *The Singer of Tales*, builds on the field research of Harvard classics professor Milman Parry in the 1930s with Yugoslavian *guslars*, contemporary bards who performed oral epics similar to those of Homer. Lord concludes that the Homeric epics were oral compositions that continued to be composed during their performance. For the *guslars* (named after the *gusle*, the one-stringed fiddle they used for accompaniment), there was no written text. The stories were performed and passed on for generations through oral tradition. Lord's discovery from Parry's documentation of the performances surpassed his original hypothesis that Homeric works contained structures of oral transmission. He states: "Oral, however, does not mean merely oral presentation. Oral epics are performed orally, it is true, but so can any other poem be performed orally. What is important is not the oral performance but rather the composition *during* oral performance" (p. 5). Lord proposes that the *guslar* as the "singer of tales" is at once the tradition and an individual creator along with the audience. He says that this role in performance does not create a conflict between preserver of tradition and creative artist; it is, rather, "one of the preservation of tradition by the constant re-creation of it" (p. 29). Lord concludes that, for the oral poet, the moment of composition is the *performance* (Albert B. Lord, *The Singer of Tales* [1960; reprint, New York: Atheneum, 1978], pp. 1-29). For a further discussion of the participation of the hearer in the creation and performance of oral poetry, see Ruth Finnegan, *Oral Poetry: Its Nature, Significance and Social Context* (Cambridge: Cambridge University Press, 1977).

An approach to texts that does not take into consideration the participation of the hearers in their performance is inadequate as a basis for a homiletic, for the omission of the hearers' participation leads to a disregard for sermon form, style, and delivery. Although Campbell notes Frei's move toward "concrete interpretive practices of the Christian community as it uses Scripture in its own life and work" (*Preaching Jesus*, p. 80), both Frei and Campbell place little emphasis on the sermon as being one of these practices. Although Campbell attempts through performance to extend the work of Frei into homiletics, he largely leaves the sermon as a performance — including the hearers' participation through its form and style — undeveloped.

CHAPTER FIVE

Clearing the Sanctuary: Room and Space

Distance Reconsidered

Among the postliberals' many challenges to Craddock's theory and method, those most pertinent to *distance* concern the hearer. Charles Campbell's first charge is about Craddock's emphasis on the hearer's experience in preaching. In *Preaching Jesus*, Campbell notes that Craddock's proposals in *As One Without Authority* and *Overhearing the Gospel* are not intended to be "full-blown homiletics" but "correctives." He also affirms Craddock's creative and positive contributions to sermon method, which include the emphasis on the hearer's participation in the sermon; the role of movement, anticipation, and concreteness; the role of the imagination; and the emphasis on the oral character of preaching. With some surprise, Campbell notes that Craddock draws on Frei's works in *Overhearing the Gospel*, where, he says, Craddock moves toward a greater appreciation of the present literary form of the canon.[1]

Campbell expresses an appreciation for Craddock's emphasis on hearer participation "to effect a new hearing of the Gospel"; nevertheless, Campbell clearly says that an "individualistic, existentialist, expe-

---

1. Charles Lamar Campbell, *Preaching Jesus: Hans Frei's Theology and the Contours of a Postliberal Theology* (Grand Rapids: Eerdmans, 1997), pp. 125-26.

riential framework remains basic to Craddock's homiletical thought."[2] Even with qualifications, both Ellingsen and Campbell place Craddock in Lindbeck's category of the experiential-expressive because of his emphasis on the experience of the hearer in the sermon. Accordingly, Ellingsen — and especially Campbell — criticize Craddock for continuing and promoting individual, private religious experience at the expense of community.

This either/or choice between experience and community has been rightly challenged by Stanley Hauerwas and L. Gregory Jones in *Why Narrative? Readings in Narrative Theology*, in which they are critical of Lindbeck's categories of experiential-expressive and cultural-linguistic for making it appear that there are only two fundamental options. Instead, as evident in the variety of their collection of essays, they propose that there are many options regarding the interrelatedness of narrative, experience, and community.[3] When the delineations between experience and participation — and between individual and community — become flexible and dynamic, Craddock need not be forced into the Procrustean bed of existential-expressivist religion.

Campbell's critique of Craddock's homiletical method exhibits an inconsistency: he criticizes Craddock's emphasis on the *experience* of the hearer, yet he praises Craddock's contribution to preaching, which includes hearer participation, movement within the sermon's form, and concreteness as a style of storytelling, imagination, and the oral nature of preaching. But all of these attributes of hearing involve the experience of the hearer. Thus, in his critique of Craddock, Campbell has created

---

2. Campbell, *Preaching Jesus*, pp. 126-27.

3. Stanley Hauerwas and L. Gregory Jones, introduction to *Why Narrative? Readings in Narrative Theology*, ed. Stanley Hauerwas and L. Gregory Jones (Grand Rapids: Eerdmans, 1989), pp. 5-9. David Ford presents an example of one such option in his essay "System, Story, Performance: A Proposal about the Role of Narrative in Christian Systematic Theology." Ford questions the strict delineation of Lindbeck's cultural-linguistic category and proposes performance as negotiating a "middle distance" between story and community. He says that "'performance,' at the cutting edge of story, has three main dynamics: praise and prayer; community life; and prophecy in word and action" (p. 191). In contrast to Campbell, Ford clearly identifies preaching as prophetic performance (David Ford, "System, Story, Performance," in Hauerwas and Jones, *Why Narrative?* pp. 191-215).

a false dichotomy between the experience of the hearer and the participation of hearers.[4] Campbell's inability to choose between the two is reflected in his omission of a sermon method that includes form, style, and delivery.

With regard to the relationship between the individual and community, Campbell's criticism of Craddock has merit. In Craddock's proposal of overhearing and distance, the focus is usually on the experience of the individual, evident by his use of the singular "listener" and "hearer." While Craddock does not develop a clear relationship between the individual and the community in *Overhearing the Gospel* (1978), he does reflect on this relationship in his earlier work *As One Without Authority* (1971), and he continues that reflection in his later book *Preaching* (1985).

The function of distance in the community can be further developed according to Craddock's understanding of the communal nature of hearing. As I discussed in chapter 3 above, Craddock's understanding of the hearer is based on the sermon as an oral/aural event. He says: "[T]he primary and fundamental nature of word is the spoken word. The spoken word is never an isolated event; it takes place where at least two or three are gathered together. It presupposes that which it also creates: community." Beginning with the premise that the spoken word is "socially owned," Craddock proposes that the sermon, when preached, is socially owned by the collective hearers, having its life and place among a group of participants who bring their "social factors" to the occasion.[5] This social ownership of the sermon, in which various social factors become a part, shows promise with respect to the function of distance and communities.

---

4. John McClure observes that Campbell's polarity between the biblical text and experience is overstated, resulting in a limited understanding of the Holy Spirit in preaching. He says that "when the interrelatedness of text and experience is denied, aspects of the illuminative work of the Holy Spirit in preaching are potentially thwarted. . . . The Holy Spirit borne witness to in the biblical text, however, is active and responsive, always challenging and transforming the textual narrative itself. Without this sense of the Spirit who lives beyond, within, and through the text, it is likely that "preaching Jesus" will mean "preaching the textuality of Jesus," or the "text-Jesus," and not "preaching the living Christ" (John S. McClure, review of Charles Lamar Campbell, *Preaching Jesus: New Directions for Homiletics in Hans Frei's Postliberal Theology, Journal for Preachers* 21, no. 2 (1998): 35.

5. Fred B. Craddock, *Preaching* (Nashville: Abingdon, 1985), pp. 31-32.

Contrary to the assumption that hearers are one community, distance provides the room (space) for not only individuals but also their respective communities to freely participate in the hearing of the gospel. Brian Blount and Leonora Tubbs Tisdale use the image of "making room at the table" for an "invitation to multicultural worship."[6] Similarly, distance can "make room" in the pulpit and the pew for the participation of communities in the hearing and creating of the sermon.

Recent Proposals

Campbell's second challenge to distance is that the hearers of sermons have changed since 1978, when Craddock first introduced his concept of overhearing. He contends that Craddock's presupposition for overhearing is that "Christendom remains alive," and thus Christian language and tradition are so familiar that they have lost their power. Therefore, Craddock's proposal of an "indirect method" as the best embodiment of stories is necessary to evoke or bring to life what is already known within the hearers. Campbell claims that Craddock's use of Kierkegaard assumes that the church in nineteenth-century Denmark is similar to his

6. Brian K. Blount and Leonora Tubbs Tisdale, eds., *Making Room at the Table: An Invitation to Multicultural Worship* (Louisville: Westminster John Knox, 2001). The basis of Tisdale's understanding of multicultural worship can be seen in *Preaching as Local Theology and Folk Art*, where she builds on Craddock's emphasis on the hearer in her aim toward "contextual preaching." She proposes that preaching as "local theology" is a "hearer-oriented" event. By contrast to speaker-oriented communication, she says that "hearer-oriented communication places primary value on the ability of the hearer to understand the message in his or her own symbolic framework, and to relate it to his or her own world" (p. 46). Drawing on Calvin's understanding of God's accommodation through language to aid in our understanding, Tisdale promotes "hearer-oriented" sermons, in which "preacher meets congregants on their ground, rather than requiring congregants to meet preacher on his or her ground" (p. 46). Contrary to Campbell's understanding of "absorption," Tisdale calls for preachers to enter, as much as possible, into the hearer's own world of symbolic understanding in the communication of the message. From this "contextual" perspective, Tisdale has questioned Campbell's homiletic, asking, "In whose language do we preach?" (Leonora Tubbs Tisdale, *Preaching as Local Theology and Folk Art* [Minneapolis: Fortress, 1997]; author interview of Leonora Tubbs Tisdale, Princeton, NJ, 1997).

own time, when "information is not what is necessary; what is needed is something else: an experience of the information we already possess."[7] Contrariwise, Campbell emphatically declares that "Christendom is dead," noting that even Craddock, in his more recent lectures, has acknowledged that congregations today are not biblically literate and that is why he emphasizes the importance of the grounding of hearers in the church's Scripture and tradition. According to Campbell, this acknowledgment undermines the presuppositions behind *As One Without Authority* and *Overhearing the Gospel*.[8] Drawing parallels between the contemporary situation of the church and the evangelism of the apostle Paul, Campbell says that Craddock's concepts of overhearing and distance are obsolete, that what we need right now is a "direct method of communication."[9]

With regard to this change in the hearer, I return to the sermon responses from students in my preaching class (at the opening of this book): "I feel crowded." "You don't know what I'm thinking!" "*You* were into the story; but *I* really don't know it" (referring to the biblical text). "Let me make my own decisions." "There was no room for me in the sermon." Sociologist of religion Robert Wuthnow — as though he were there in my classroom describing my students — notes that contemporary young adults are no longer joiners who are guided and informed by institutions, including the church. By contrast, he describes young adults' approach to religion, spirituality, and life in general as "tinkering." "Tinkerers" piece together thoughts about religion and interests in spirituality from a "plethora of activities" and the "resources at hand." Wuthnow aptly describes the hearing ethos in my current preaching classes: "Each person is a tinkerer. Each individual claims the authority — in fact, the duty — to make up his or her mind about what to believe...."[10] The current hearer

---

7. Craddock, *Overhearing*, pp. 22, 104; Campbell's summary in *Preaching Jesus*, p. 127.

8. Craddock, "The Sermon as Twice-told Tale," Sprunt Lectures, Union Theological Seminary, Richmond, VA, Feb. 4-6, 1991, quoted in Campbell, *Preaching Jesus*, p.128.

9. Campbell, *Preaching Jesus*, pp. 127-28.

10. Robert Wuthnow, *After the Baby Boomers: How Twenty- and Thirty-Somethings Are Shaping the Future of American Religion* (Princeton, NJ: Princeton University Press, 2007), pp. 13-16.

approaches the sermon with a critical distance and often a distance of un-familiarity with the biblical story. In his call for replacing overhearing and distance, Campbell rightly observes that the hearers of sermons have significantly changed during the last thirty-five years. However, it is this very change in hearing that has prompted the embracing of distance in more recent homiletics.

Charles Bartow: Distance in Conversation

Writing from a background in speech communication and theology, Charles Bartow notes the shift away from public speaking as "declamation," a sender-receiver style of communication in which an active speaker announces and a passive listener receives. In a declamatory style, the dynamic is one-way, from sender to receiver, where the aim of communication is overcoming the distance between the speaker and the hearer. Acknowledging that the declamatory style may be impressive, dramatic, and even convincing, Bartow rejects it as "totally inappropriate for use in the proclamation of the gospel." Instead, he proposes "conversation" as a style most fitting to preaching — in which mutual participation occurs in the speaking event. Bartow's understanding of preaching as conversation is especially appropriate to the contemporary hearer. In conversation, there is no assumed "aesthetic distance" between the hearer and the preacher to be overcome through the sermon. "On the contrary," he observes, "the speakers, as it were, stand *with* their listeners, receiving and responding to whatever it is they are met to consider."

For Bartow, the sermon as conversation provides room for the "personal, unique, and perhaps even idiosyncratic perception" of the preacher.[11] In contrast to a declamatory style, conversation also creates room for var-

---

11. Charles L. Bartow, *The Preaching Moment: A Guide to Sermon Delivery* (Dubuque: Kendall Hunt, 1995), pp. 64, 59. Just as in Craddock's theological grounding for style, Bartow's *The Preaching Moment* places distance in the theological context of conversation. For Bartow, the sermon as conversation is based on doctrines of creation and incarnation, the "world-creating Word of God and our own world-creating word being present and resonant in Christ." In this conversation, "Word," "words," and "worlds" come together in what Bartow calls the "preaching moment" (p. 59).

ied perceptions and responses by the hearer. Aware of the changing sense of authority in contemporary communication, Bartow says, "[t]he preacher will leave the listeners free to respond on the basis of their own 'insight and sense of the truth.'"[12] As with Craddock's proposal, a benefit of room for the hearer is free participation.

David Buttrick: Distance and Perspective

Whereas Craddock and Bartow present a change in hearing in the communication event, David Buttrick addresses a shift of consciousness in the contemporary hearer as a change of perception. In *Homiletic: Moves and Structures*, he presents distance as a "point of view," a "perspective" that is based on the contemporary consciousness of the congregation.[13] In his later book *A Captive Voice: The Liberation of Preaching*, Buttrick says that "nowadays, people think through imaging," and thus he argues that, because "thinking" has changed in the congregation over the last thirty years, so must homiletics.[14]

This change of "thinking" in the consciousness of the congregation becomes the basis for Buttrick's use of distance when preaching from the parables. Drawing on Craddock's *Overhearing the Gospel*, Buttrick's "hermeneutical strategy" is that parables are best overheard. By "standing back," the preacher creates the critical distance necessary to see a parable as a progression of episodic images. When the preacher presents these images in the sermon, a separation occurs in which the preacher is viewing and considering the story "beside" the congregation.[15] This distance is beneficial to the text because such an interpretative "posture" (Craddock's term for distance) permits the parable to "unfold in the con-

---

12. Herbert H. Farmer, *Servant of the Word* (Philadelphia: Fortress, 1964), p. 49, quoted in Bartow, *Preaching Moment*, p. 64.

13. David Buttrick, *Homiletic: Moves and Structures* (Philadelphia: Fortress, 1988), pp. 40-43, 77-79.

14. David Buttrick, *A Captive Voice: The Liberation of Preaching* (Louisville: Westminster John Knox, 1994), p. 99.

15. For Buttrick's discussion of "standing back" and "considering" as a "stage of consciousness" of a text or situation, see *Homiletic*, p. 323.

sciousness, episode by episode, doing what it is designed to do."[16] Distance is also beneficial to the congregation, for when the preacher is not preaching *at* the congregation, the congregation and the preacher might react to the story *together.*

Quoting playwright and director Bertolt Brecht (discussed in chapter 2), Buttrick says that the "moves" within parables are "closer to sharply defined scenes in a drama than to the smoothed-out flow of storytelling."[17] As Brecht used "alienation devices" to separate the audience from the play, so Buttrick promotes a separation of the congregation from the parable. The result is that distance creates the "imaginative space" required for the parable to "do what it may want to do" — and for the responses of the congregation and the preacher. In Buttrick's proposal of distance, the preacher's question "What am I going to preach on?" is replaced with the question from the pulpit and the pew, "What's going on here?"[18]

Although it is evident that Craddock has influenced Buttrick's understanding of distance, there remain significant differences between the two proposals. For Craddock, distance is a dynamic *among* the text, preacher, and listener. For Buttrick, distance is a dynamic *within* the consciousness of the preacher and congregation with respect to the text. Whereas Craddock emphasizes the interplay between hearing and speaking, Buttrick addresses a changed consciousness whose focus is on images and emotions.

Jana Childers: Distance and Spiritual Space

Whereas Buttrick perceives distance as a function of consciousness, Jana Childers discusses distance as an element of performance. In *Performing the Word: Preaching as Theatre,* Childers quotes anthropologist Victor Turner, who writes, "Religion, like art, lives in so far as it is performed."[19] Noting that both preaching and theater share the importance given to the

16. Buttrick, *Captive Voice,* p. 98.

17. Bertolt Brecht, *Brecht on Theatre: The Development of an Aesthetic,* trans. John Willett (New York: Hill and Wang, 1966), quoted in Buttrick, *Captive Voice,* p. 98.

18. Buttrick, *Captive Voice,* pp. 98-99; see also Buttrick, *Homiletic,* p. 352.

19. Victor Turner, *From Ritual to Theatre: The Human Seriousness of Play* (New York: PAJ Publications, 1982), p. 86, quoted in Jana Childers, *Performing the Word: Preaching*

meaning of space, Childers characterizes distance in preaching as physical, psychological, aesthetic, and spiritual.

From analyzing the use of space in the theater, Childers observes that the first use of distance in preaching is practical, the separation of the congregation in order to see. The second use is functional: a raised pulpit not only enables sight, it also creates an "arena" for the preacher or audience. The pulpit in the sanctuary functions like the theater's proscenium arch, where the spatial distance of the congregation creates a focus on a "common picture." The result is that the congregation is unified, corporately creating space for "something to happen" (pp. 45-46).

Childers proposes that the third function of distance is psychological. Distance between the congregation and preacher functions under the same principle as the distance between therapist and client. Using psychologist James Hillman's term, she characterizes distance as "negative capability," the "withdrawing" of the listener in order to "make room for the other to become present":

> In this way, we may see what is perhaps the most important of the roles distance plays in theatre and preaching. Aesthetic distance creates psychological or spiritual space. The line of demarcation that separates the preacher and the congregation makes it possible for the person in the pew to have her own experience. Literal space makes figurative space possible. (p. 46)

Using the terms "psychological" and "spiritual" interchangeably, Childers observes that aesthetic distance in preaching creates a "psychological or spiritual space" that "facilitates belief." Childers's fourth function of distance is thus spiritual. "Detachment" allows the person in the pew to close the gap between himself or herself and the preacher. In this "choice," says Childers, is the "seed of belief" (p. 47).

As if in reply to the student who said, "There was no room for me in the sermon," Childers calls for preaching that creates sacred space for the "other to become present," in which the hearer has "choice."

---

as *Theatre* (Nashville: Abingdon Press, 1998), p. 47. Hereafter, page references to this latter work appear in parentheses in the text.

Conclusion

During an interview with Fred Craddock, I asked: "In light of the changes in the last twenty years of the person in the pew, is there anything you would change about 'distance' from the book's [*Overhearing the Gospel*] first edition?" Without missing a beat, Craddock replied, "It helps to know the stories."[20]

The subtitle of the first edition of *Overhearing the Gospel* (1978) was *Preaching and Teaching the Faith to Persons Who Have Heard It All Before.* The book was reissued in 2002 as simply *Overhearing the Gospel*, with that initial subtitle dropped. My endeavor in this book has been a reclaiming of distance in preaching for contemporary hearers, for those who have *never heard* it before. In his 1991 Sprunt lectures, Craddock argues that the change in biblical literacy *requires* preaching that involves the experience of the hearer.[21] I should note that Craddock does not say that only overhearing or distance is to be used in preaching. Craddock's method encourages a combination of indirect and direct communication, overhearing and hearing, distance and participation — often via a combination of storytelling and directly speaking to the hearer. In this combination, overhearing can effect a "first hearing."

I had the opportunity to experience such a first hearing when, as a visitor, I attended a worship service on an Easter Sunday. The young man sitting next to me in the pew was also a visitor, but it was clear from his mannerisms that, unlike me, he was unfamiliar with worship. He was visiting his daughter, an eight-year-old and a regular attendee of church school, and he kept looking to her for directions as to what to do next in the service. During the reading of Luke's Gospel, I did not notice the man's reactions, nor was I aware of him during the following anthem, but when the preacher stepped to the center of the chancel and proceeded to retell the Easter story, I could not help but overhear his responses as I was facing forward and listening to the preacher. When the preacher reached the part of the story where the women find an empty tomb, and men in dazzling

20. Author interview of Fred Craddock, 1998. This interview was conducted twenty years after the first printing of *Overhearing the Gospel* (1978).
21. Craddock, "The Sermon as Twice-told Tale."

clothes say, "He is not here," the man gasped, turned to his daughter, and asked in a whisper, "Where was he?" I was relieved and encouraged that the sermon did not end with the retelling of the biblical story. As if in reply to the man's question, the preacher continued the sermon and the story by directly proclaiming to the congregation, "He is here!"

As listeners overhear the story, distance provides the room for responses by those who have never heard the story before, or who are simply listening for the first time. Combined with the participation of direct address, a first hearing may become a new hearing of the gospel.

"*There Is a Wideness in God's Mercy*"[22]

As I have said at the outset, the aims of this book have been to contribute to a greater understanding of distance in the field of homiletics; to equip teachers and students of preaching to return to the classroom with an informed ability to evaluate distance in sermon form, style, and delivery; and to encourage preachers (including me) to acquire greater understanding and skill in the use of distance in the creation and preaching of sermons. In my endeavors to research through practice, I am presenting the following two sermons in which I use distance in biblical interpretation and sermon construction. I offer them as neither illustrations nor models but as grateful responses to the "wideness in God's mercy" that creates room for us to speak the gospel — and the space for the gospel to be freely heard.

---

22. Frederick William Faber, "There Is a Wideness in God's Mercy" (1854), *The Presbyterian Hymnal: Hymns, Psalms, and Spiritual Songs* (Louisville: Westminster John Knox, 1990), p. 298.

Two Sermons

"Were You There?"

"The Crucifixion of Jesus according to John"

John 19:16b-25

Were you there when they crucified my Lord?
　　Were you *there?*
Were you there when they nailed him to a tree?
　　Were *we* there?

I used to be chaplain of Centre College in Kentucky. One Good Friday, as I was on my way to lead the chapel service (very much like this one today), I ran into a student going in the opposite direction.

"Are you coming to the service?" I asked in my most nonthreatening, nonjudgmental, invitational-yet-giving-the-student-freedom-to-choose . . . chaplain sort of way.

"No," he said, as if to say, "And that's final!"

It was not his answer but his tone that took me by surprise. I knew him to be a believer and an active member of our college fellowship. I also knew

Preached on Good Friday, April 10, 2009, Millar Chapel, Princeton Theological Seminary.

him to be a person of depth, and I thought that he must have put some thought into his answer. *Why not?* I wondered.

Perhaps he read my face, or perhaps he wanted to explain. As if hearing my unvoiced question, he replied: "I'm not into make-believe. I'm not into pretending that *I* was *there.*"

Were we there? Can we be?

I think about his answer every Good Friday. What are we doing here today? Is this merely the land of make-believe? Are we in a kind of religious, musical period piece of Bibleland? Is this the church's version of the "time tunnel"?

Were we there when they nailed him to a tree?

John, in his telling the story of Jesus' crucifixion, seems to speak directly to this student — and perhaps to us as well. John seems less interested in telling the story in a way that makes us feel we are there. In reverse, John asks:

Where is Christ now? Who is Christ now?

And, as we face the crucifixion of our Lord,

Where are we . . . now?

In the other three Gospels, the crucifixion is portrayed with such detail, the pictures painted so vividly, that we can't help but be drawn into the story.

In Luke's telling, we find ourselves up close to the cross, perhaps too close:

Side speared. Stretched on wood.
"Shouting." "Scoffing." "Crying out." "Breathing."

The Christ who identified himself with the suffering of others now suffers himself. And we are close, so close that, with the women, we want to wail and beat our breasts in sorrow over what we see — over what they have done to our Lord.

In Luke, oh yes, we are there, and we tremble.

149

But we are not encouraged to wail in John. The crucifixion is told with little description, with only essential detail. The scene is simple, almost spare: it keeps us at a distance. It's as if John doesn't want us to get so involved in the drama of the cross *then* that we lose the cross's meaning — for *today*.

In Mark, we aren't quite as close to the cross as in Luke, but we are still there. Keeping a safe distance, we watch as Jesus is spit on, humiliated, mocked as a king on a cross:

> Bleeding barbs of thorns. Biting blades of words.
> "He saved others; he can't save himself."
> "Messiah, King — yeah, right! Come on down! When we see it, we'll
>   believe it."

And in fear, shame, and despair, we cover our eyes and cower over the tragedy of the death of our leader, our Lord. Who was he? And what will become of us?

But not in John. In John's Gospel we know who he is. What is mockery in Mark, a sign above Jesus' head that reads, "King of the Jews," in John is a profound truth, written in Aramaic, Roman, and Greek for all the world to read: "The king of the Jews." And we recognize the king of the world. In John, the identity of the one on the cross is not a mystery. We know who he is from the beginning of that Gospel:

> the beginning Word
> the creating Word
> the Word of light and life itself

And we know who he is from the very beginnings of the church:

> God of God, Light of Light, Very God of Very God.
> Christ. King. Savior.

For John's community — and for ours — the cross is not a tragedy, for we know who he is and why he came.

In Matthew's telling of the crucifixion story, there is so much dialogue and defense that it sounds like a great courtroom where everyone is on trial — everyone, that is, but Jesus.

> With the Sanhedrin, the religious leaders are on trial.
> The disciples, especially Peter and Judas, are on trial.
> With Pilate and the soldiers, Rome is on trial.
> In calling for Barabbas over Jesus, the people are on trial.
> And, at the cross, *we* are on trial.

But not so in John. In his Gospel, Jesus is the one on trial, and not by an earthly court. Jesus' trial, Jesus' test, is one of obedience to God's will, one of following that will — even to his death.

Here, in John's Gospel, there is no Simon of Cyrene to carry Jesus' cross. John says that he carried the cross "by himself" to Golgotha, the place of the skull. The wood of the cross in John is not the executioner's tree, nor is it a wooden yoke forced upon him. In John, the wood is a shepherd's staff, cracked into a cross, a sign that the good shepherd will choose to do anything for the sheep, will even die for the sheep, that they might live. And we, like Peter, are told to feed the sheep, tend the sheep. Even if it leads to death of self and body.

Jesus' words echo from the cross today:

> If you love me, you will obey me.
> Take up your cross and follow me.
>> Follow me to mission.
>> Follow me to community.
>> Follow me to homelessness.
>> Follow me to shelter.
> Follow me to work.
> Follow me to purpose.
> Follow me to out-of-work.
> Follow me to searching.
>> Follow me to home.
>> Follow me to relationships.
>> Follow me to loss.

Follow me to loneliness.
    Follow me to illness.
    Follow me to wholeness.
    Follow me to death.
    Follow me to hope.
    Follow me to *life*.

Because he was there, we are here. And because he is here:

We can follow. We *can* follow. We can *follow* . . .

"Sibling Revelry"

Luke 15:11-32

It was the final gathering of pastors at the Joe R. Engle Institute of Preaching. I look forward to this institute all year, when those who have been in ministry for at least two years come to be better preachers; that is, to become better at proclaiming the gospel in their particular communities. I look forward to this gathering of preachers because they know what they know, and they know what they don't know — and they want your help. Yet I'm kept humble by the attendees such as the pastor who said, "They really should teach a speech course like this at Princeton Seminary." Turns out, he was one of my students in the required year-long course in speech at Princeton Seminary.

It was at this final gathering that Dean James Kay, quoting James Forbes, said that preachers need to be "called" and "re-called." As Dean Kay continued, an irreverent reverend next to me whispered in my ear, "That could be taken two different ways." Disguising a chuckle as a cough, I realized he was right. Whether a preacher is re-called or *re*called depends on how it is said and how it is heard. It depends on the tone of voice.

In the parable about the prodigal son and his older brother, we have images and tones for characters who are both re-called and *re*called. We often think of this story in terms of plot. However, when reading the text aloud, I found myself focusing on the eye and the ear. Helmut Thielicke said that "parables are the picture book of God" — and I would add, "with sound."

The images in the first half of the parable are like familiar portraits hung on the wall, scenes embellished with depictions ranging from church school curriculum to Rembrandt paintings. The first frame is the cocky pose of the younger sibling, straight-eyed asking — or rather, demanding — his inheritance via the selling of property. Seen through our eyes,

---

Preached at Opening Communion Service, September 19, 2011, Millar Chapel, Princeton Theological Seminary.

where parents are expected to jeopardize their future financial security by sending their youngest on their way — to college or grad school or seminary — we may miss the first-century recognition of a scene set for financial and family ruin. Property was security, and children guaranteed the future. They were needed to work. And they were needed to eventually run things and keep things going. I was struck by one painting of this scene where, in the corner of the house, was the mother, knitting, with the anxious face of one who is powerless during a transaction between father and son that would change the life of her family forever. As for the tone of asking for your inheritance ahead of time? You might as well say your father is dead — to his face. Try to say *that* out loud, using the names of your own parents, to get a taste of the impact of this scene.

The picture in the next frame is abstract, dark, and cloudy: you can't really make out any figures. The title underneath reads "Squandering Wealth in Dissolute Living," a picture kept pretty vague by Jesus the narrator, but one that is fleshed out with detail in the imagination of the older brother: "Your son devoured your property with prostitutes." I might add that this section was pretty fleshed out in the imaginations of some commentators as well.

The next portrait is that of a gaunt, broken, lonely, lifeless-looking shell of a man bent over a pigsty, a sign recognized by ancient eyes, older than our own, as insult added to injury, ultimate debasement — a place where things couldn't get any worse.

But when the father enters the picture, it's like the great wall of Hogwarts in a Harry Potter movie, where the characters go back and forth as they enter living scenes in picture frames. Instead of creating new portraits, it's as if the father enters all three: inverting, flipping, smudging out, and painting over. The straight-eyed demanding pose of the younger son has now become averted eyes and an attempt to kneel, an attempt that fails because of the father's clutching embrace that is not ready to let go.

When the father enters the portrait of the murky shadows of "dissolute living," he does not clean it up, whitewash it over, or discreetly turn it toward the wall. He splashes it with color and sound: details of an extravagant banquet with music and dancing, prompted by his call, "Let's eat and celebrate!" This is more than a dinner party; and it's more than cranking up the Black Eyed Peas (sorry, that's the best I can do). I would paint this party as a potlatch, a festal ceremony of the Native Americans of my childhood home, the Pacific Northwest, where the host gives extravagant gifts to all the guests. *Potlatch* — even the name itself means to "give away," or "a gift." In fact, it has been legally banned in some places because the hosts would literally give away everything they owned.

And when the father enters the next portrait, it's as if the negative space has been inverted: the once exposed outline of a hungry, jagged body is now filled, fully enveloped by a parent's embrace. Rags are painted over with a robe of the honored guest at a feast. Prohibited pigs give way to a succulent calf. Ring and shoes are detailed onto hands and feet — blotting out any conditions for full family membership. As for the sound of the scene, some writers want you to choose between two options regarding the *tone* of the younger son: on the one side, an earnest confession of a contrite heart and, like the publican, the sound of sincere remorse, "Lord, forgive me, a sinner"; or, on the other side, the portrayal of an opportunist pure and simple. Or, in the extreme, a caricature of someone from an episode of *Jersey Shore*: "Whoa, I mus' be crazy stayin' here — they gotta sweet deal at home."

His confession was probably like ours, a mixture of remorse and desperation — the sound of homesickness. Either way, it doesn't matter. The father ignores the son's rehearsed speech, interrupting it with shouts for restoration and celebration. I never really appreciated this interruption until I read it aloud. You don't necessarily see it on the page, but you can hear it: the only requirement of the lost to be found is being found — being there.

Searching. Running. Embracing. Celebrating. These images are familiar, and they need to be, until they become familiar gestures of our congregations. But what surprised me in the second half of the story was how unfamiliar I was with the older brother. Not so much with the *image:* two silhouettes against the dusky sky outside the house, one sulking, the other pleading — I was familiar enough with that image. But I was unfamiliar with the elder son's *voice.* When "taking on" his voice, one may find it too easy to set him up.

In performance studies, we say that there are flat characters and round characters. "Flat" doesn't mean monotone, or with no emotion; it means that emotions and voice are staged, set, and predictable. If it's a flat character in a morality play, once you learn the lesson ("Don't be like the self-righteous older brother; be like the welcoming father"), you can easily throw that character away. If it's a melodrama, the preacher's rant against the grudge-bearing son is good entertainment, and when the entertainment is over, one can easily dismiss him. Both have nothing to do with the rounded characters in our lives, including ourselves.

So, in order for us to better understand the elder brother's complaint, I offer some complaints that I've heard about homecomings from being a pastor, a teacher, a family member, and a friend. One young woman was planning her wedding. After not hearing from her father since he had abandoned his family thirteen years earlier, she was told by her mother that he would like to attend the ceremony. He realized it probably would be "too much" to escort his daughter down the aisle, but he wanted to know whether he could attend. The tone of the bride's voice was filled with anger and hurt: "After thirteen years, how dare he!"

I've heard the conversation of a sister and a brother about their other sister, who never once visited their dying mother but shows up at the funeral asking about the divvying up of her mother's furniture:

"What did she ever do?"

"She has her nerve, coming in here like that."

I've heard a father spit out his inner turmoil when the son who stole from the family business wants to return for Christmas dinner. "Not at my table," mutters the father.

Perhaps by hearing a little more clearly the true anger and resentment of the prodigal's older brother, we might know how hard it would be to step inside that door — to join the party. And we might understand a little better why the father had to plead.

I've heard Michelle Shocked sing her complaint against the whole story:

What's to be done with a prodigal son?
Welcome him home with open arms
Throw a big party, invite your friends
Our boy's come back home.

When a girl goes home with the oats she's sown
It's draw your shades and your shutters
She's bringing such shame to the family name
The return of the prodigal daughter.

I've heard a woman in her thirties tell me of her seventeen-year-old daughter, who appeared out of the blue one day on her doorstep. Seventeen years ago, as a teenager, she had given up her infant daughter for adoption. Now she could hardly wait to introduce her daughter to her church, not only to her friends but also to the young women she taught in church school. After that Sunday, she was called in and "gently notified" that there had been complaints. It was no longer appropriate for her to serve as a teacher, for she would not be a good role model for young women. She told me: "I was so naïve. I was so excited about finding my daughter and bringing her to church, it didn't even occur to me there would be a problem." She and her daughter were inside celebrating, whereas the congregation was out in the fields — work, work, work.

The truth is that most of us are the older sibling in the story, or we wouldn't be here today: responsibly following the rules, steps, procedures, and exams (and expecting others to do so); making up for a lack of joy with discipline, and for a lack of God's presence with productivity. And when we are "prone to wander, Lord, I feel it," we forget it's to leave the one we "love." So we bury our hoes all the deeper in the same place — work, work, work. Perhaps one of the reasons the older son is *here*, while the party is going on *over there*, is not a matter of principle. He just can't dance. He never learned how, never had the time.

Sometimes it takes an unabashed celebration of salvation to remind us that we've worked ourselves into a far-off place. And that we need to be *re*called in order to be re-called.

We who are working in the fields of faith are met by the host of the potlatch, who says: "All that is mine is yours. I've already given it all away. I gave you my son. But there is a celebration for all who were dead — and all who are dead inside — to come to life. We have to celebrate! We may even have to dance!"

[Drumbeats are heard in the background.]
    Do you hear the tones? The opening wide of doors?
    The snap of bread, splash of wine? Songs at the supper table?
    In the words of the host,
        "Let's eat and celebrate!"

Bibliography

Abrams, M. H. *A Glossary of Literary Terms*. Fort Worth: Harcourt Brace, 1999.

Achtemeier, Paul. "How Adequate is the New Hermeneutic?" *Theology Today* 23, no. 1 (April 1966): 101-19.

Adorno, Theodor W. *Aesthetic Theory*. Translated by Robert Hullot-Kentor. Minneapolis: University of Minnesota Press, 1997.

Allen, Ronald J. "Modes of Discourse for the Sermon in the Postmodern World." In *Theology for Preaching: Authority, Truth, and Knowledge of God in a Postmodern Ethos*, edited by Ronald J. Allen, Barbara Shires Blaisdell, and Scott Black Johnston. Nashville: Abingdon, 1997.

————. *Patterns of Preaching: A Sermon Sampler*. St Louis: Chalice Press, 1998.

Allison, Henry E. *Kant's Theory of Taste: A Reading of the Critique of Aesthetic Judgment*. Cambridge: Cambridge University Press, 2001.

Armstrong, Chloe, and Paul D. Brandes. *The Oral Interpretation of Literature*. New York: McGraw-Hill, 1963.

Auerbach, Erich. *Mimesis: The Representation of Reality in Western Literature*. Translated by Willard R. Trask. Princeton, NJ: Princeton University Press, 1953.

Bacon, Wallace A. *The Art of Interpretation*. New York: Holt, Rinehart, and Winston, 1979.

————. "The Dangerous Shores: From Elocution to Interpretation." *Quarterly Journal of Speech* 46, no. 2 (April 1960): 148-52.

Bacon, Wallace A., and Robert S. Breen. *Literature as Experience*. New York: McGraw-Hill, 1959.

Bailey, James L., and Lyle D. Vander Broek. *Literary Forms in the New Testament*. Louisville: Westminster John Knox, 1992.

Barilli, Renato. *Rhetoric*. Translated by Guiliana Menozzi. Minneapolis: University of Minnesota Press, 1989.

Bartlett, David. "Story and History: Narratives and Claims." *Interpretation* 55, no. 3 (July 1991): 229-40.

Bartow, Charles L. *An Evaluation of Student Preaching in the Basic Homiletics Courses at Princeton Theological Seminary: A Farmerian Approach to Homiletical Criticism.* PhD dissertation, New York University, 1971.

———. "In Service to the Servants of the Word: Teaching Speech at Princeton Seminary." *Princeton Seminary Bulletin* 13, no. 3 (1992): 275-86.

———. *God's Human Speech: A Practical Theology of Proclamation.* Grand Rapids: Eerdmans, 1997.

———. *The Preaching Moment: A Guide to Sermon Delivery.* Nashville: Abingdon Preacher's Library, 1981.

———. *The Preaching Moment: A Guide to Sermon Delivery.* Dubuque: Kendall/Hunt Publishing, 1995.

———. *The Preaching Moment: A Hands-On Speech Course for Scripture Reading and Preaching,* no. 6, *Nonverbal Communication.* Princeton: PTS Media, Princeton Theological Seminary, 1998. Videocassette.

Beardslee, William A. *Literary Criticism of the New Testament.* Philadelphia: Fortress, 1970.

Beardsley, Monroe C. "The Aesthetic Point of View." In *Art and Interpretation: An Anthology of Readings in Aesthetics and the Philosophy of Art,* edited by Eric Dayton. Toronto, Ontario: Broadview Press, 1998.

———. *The Aesthetic Point of View: Selected Essays.* Edited by Michael J. Wreen and Donald M. Callen. Ithaca: Cornell University Press, 1982.

———. *Aesthetics from Classical Greece to the Present: A Short History.* New York: Macmillan, 1966.

Beecher, Lyman. Bibliography of the Lyman Beecher Lectureship on Preaching. Yale Divinity School: http://www.library.yale.edu (accessed January 2012).

Beinecke Rare Book and Manuscript Library, Yale University: http://www.yale.edu (accessed January 2012).

Beloof, Robert. *The Performing Voice in Literature.* Boston: Little, Brown, 1966.

Berleant, Arnold. *Art and Engagement.* Philadelphia: Temple University Press, 1991.

———. Aesthetics Beyond the Arts. Burlington, VT: Ashgate, 2012.

Black, Edwin. *Rhetorical Criticism: A Study in Method.* Madison: University of Wisconsin Press, 1978.

———. *Rhetorical Questions: Studies of Public Discourse.* Chicago: University of Chicago Press, 1992.

Blount, Brian K., and Leonora Tubbs Tisdale, eds. *Making Room at the Table: An Invitation to Multicultural Worship.* Louisville: Westminster John Knox, 2001.

Boomershine, Thomas E. *Story Journey: An Invitation to the Gospel as Storytelling.* Nashville: Abingdon, 1988.

Booth, Wayne C. *The Rhetoric of Fiction.* Chicago: University of Chicago Press, 1983.

Booth, Wayne C., and Marshall W. Gregory. *Rhetoric: Writing as Thinking/Thinking as Writing*. New York: Harper and Row, 1987.

Bozarth-Campbell, Alla. *The Word's Body: An Incarnational Aesthetic of Interpretation*. Tuscaloosa: University of Alabama Press, 1979.

Brack, Harold A. *Effective Oral Interpretation for Religious Leaders*. Englewood Cliffs, NJ: Prentice-Hall, 1964.

Brecht, Bertolt. *Collected Plays*. Vol. 3, Pt. 1. Translated by Ralph Manheim, edited by John Willett and Ralph Manheim. London: Methuen, 1991.

———. "Short Description of a New Technique of Acting Which Produces an Alienation Effect." In *The Twentieth Century Performance Reader*, edited by Michael Huxley and Noel Witts. New York: Routledge, 1996.

Breen, Robert S. *Chamber Theatre*. Englewood Cliffs, NJ: Prentice-Hall, 1978.

Brock, Bernard L., Robert L. Scott, and James W. Chesbro, eds. *Methods of Rhetorical Criticism: A Twentieth-Century Perspective*. Detroit: Wayne State University Press, 1990.

Brockett, Oscar. *The Essential Theatre*. New York: Holt, Rinehart and Winston, 1988.

Brooks, Keith, Eugene Bahn, and L. LaMont Okey. *The Communicative Act of Oral Interpretation*. Boston: Allyn and Bacon, 1976.

Brown, Frank Burch. *Religious Aesthetics: A Theological Study of Making and Meaning*. Princeton, NJ: Princeton University Press, 1989.

Brown, John Russell, ed. *The Oxford Illustrated History of Theatre*. Oxford: Oxford University Press, 1997.

Brown, Robert McAfee. "My Story and 'The Story.'" *Theology Today* 32, no. 1 (April-January 1975-76): 166-73.

Brueggemann, Walter. *The Threat of Life: Sermons on Pain, Power, and Weakness*. Edited by Charles L. Campbell. Minneapolis: Fortress, 1996.

Bullock, Jeffrey F. "Preaching in a Postmodern Wor[l]d: Gadamer's Philosophical Hermeneutics as Homiletical Conversation." AAR/SBL Christian Theological Research Group, November 22, 1997: http://home.apu.edu/~CTRF/papers/1997_papers/bullock.html (accessed September 2001).

Bullough, Edward. *Aesthetics: Lectures and Essays*. Stanford: Stanford University Press, 1957.

———. "Psychical Distance." In *A Modern Book of Esthetics*, edited by Melvin Rader. New York: Holt, Rinehart, and Winston, 1979.

———. "'Psychical Distance' as a Factor in Art and an Aesthetic Principle." *British Journal of Psychology* 5 (June 1912): 87-118. Reprinted in *Aesthetics: Lectures and Essays*. Stanford: Stanford University Press, 1957.

Buttrick, David. *A Captive Voice: The Liberation of Preaching*. Louisville: Westminster John Knox Press, 1994.

———. *Homiletic: Moves and Structures*. Philadelphia: Fortress, 1988.

————. *Speaking Parables: A Homiletic Guide.* Louisville: Westminster John Knox, 2000.

————. "Who Is Listening?" In *Listening to the Word: Studies in Honor of Fred B. Craddock,* edited by Gail R. O'Day and Thomas G. Long. Nashville: Abingdon, 1993.

Calin, William. "Erich Auerbach's Mimesis — 'Tis Fifty Years Since: A Reassessment." *Style* (Fall 1999): http://www.findarticles.com (accessed October 2002).

Campbell, Charles Lamar. Interview by author. Columbia Theological Seminary, Decatur, GA, 1998.

————. "More Than Quandaries: Character Ethics and Preaching." *Journal for Preachers* 16, no. 4 (1993): 31-37.

————. "Performing the Scriptures: Preaching and Jesus' 'Third Way.'" *Journal for Preachers* 17, no. 2 (1994): 18-24.

————. "Preaching Jesus: Hans Frei's Theology and the Contours of a Postliberal Homiletic." PhD dissertation, Duke University, 1993.

————. *Preaching Jesus: New Directions for Homiletics in Hans Frei's Postliberal Theology.* Grand Rapids: Eerdmans, 1997.

————. Review of *Theology and Narrative: Selected Essays,* by Hans Frei. *Modern Theology* 10 (October 1994): 425-27.

————. "Theological Table Talk. A Not-So-Distant Mirror: Nineteenth Century Popular Fiction and Pulpit Storytelling." *Theology Today* 51, no. 4 (January 1995): 574-83.

Carroll, Noël. "Art and Interaction." *Journal of Aesthetics and Art Criticism* 45, no. 1 (Fall 1986): 57-68.

————. *Philosophy of Art: A Contemporary Introduction.* New York: Routledge, Taylor, and Francis Group, 2002.

Carter, Joan. "The Role of the Arts in Worship." In *Postmodern Worship and the Arts,* edited by Doug Adams and Michael E. Moynahan, S.J. San Jose: Resource Publications, 2002.

Cavarero, Adriana. *Relating Narratives: Storytelling and Selfhood.* Translated by Paul A. Kottman. London: Routledge, 1997.

Childers, Jana. *Performing the Word: Preaching as Theatre.* Nashville: Abingdon, 1998.

Childers, Jana, and Clayton J. Schmit, eds. *Performance in Preaching: Bringing the Sermon to Life.* Grand Rapids: Baker Academic, 2008.

Cohen, Ted, and Paul Guyer. "Introduction to Kant's Aesthetics." In *Aesthetics: A Critical Anthology,* edited by George Dickie, Richard Sclafani, and Ronald Roblin. New York: St. Martin's Press, 1989.

Conquergood, Dwight. "Boasting in Anglo-Saxon England: Performance and the Heroic Ethos." *Literature in Performance* 1, no. 2 (April 1981): 24-34.

——. "Rethinking Ethnography: Towards a Critical Cultural Politics." *Communication Monographs* 58 (June 1991): 179-94.

Craddock, Fred B. *As One Without Authority.* Nashville: Abingdon Press, 1971.

——. *As One Without Authority.* 2nd edition. St. Louis: Chalice Press, 2001.

——. "But If Someone Rises from the Grave." The Mullen Lectures, Southern Baptist Theological Seminary, Louisville, KY, 1987. Cassette.

——. "Can I Also Be Included?" Lecture at Candler School of Theology, Emory University, Atlanta, GA, November 14, 1985. Cassette.

——. *The Cherry Log Sermons.* Louisville: Westminster John Knox, 2001.

——. *Craddock Stories.* Edited by Mike Graves and Richard F. Ward. St. Louis: Chalice Press, 2001.

——. *The Gospels.* Nashville: Abingdon, 1981.

——. "If at the Altar You Remember." Sermon at Fifth Avenue Presbyterian Church, New York, NY, August 13, 1989. Cassette.

——. Author interview of Fred Craddock. Columbia Theological Seminary, Decatur, GA, 1998.

——. "Is There Still Room for Rhetoric?" In *Preaching on the Brink: The Future of Homiletics,* edited by Martha F. Simmons, pp. 66-74. Nashville: Abingdon, 1996.

——. *John.* John Knox Preaching Guides, edited by John H. Hayes. Atlanta: John Knox Press, 1982.

——. Lecture at Candler School of Theology, Emory University, Atlanta, GA, 1984.

——. *Luke.* Interpretation: A Bible Commentary for Teaching and Preaching, edited by James L. Mays, Patrick D. Miller, and Paul J. Achtemeier. Louisville: Westminster John Knox, 1990.

——. "Occasion-Text-Sermon: A Case Study." *Interpretation* 35, no. 1 (January 1981): 59-71.

——. "Overhearing the Gospel: The Illusion of Truth without Imagination." The Lyman Beecher Lectures, Yale Divinity School, New Haven, CT, 1978. Cassette.

——. *Overhearing the Gospel: Preaching and Teaching the Faith to Persons Who Have Heard It All Before.* Nashville: Abingdon Press, 1986.

——. *Overhearing the Gospel.* 2nd edition. St. Louis: Chalice Press, 2002.

——. *Philippians.* Interpretation: A Bible Commentary for Teaching and Preaching, edited by James L. Mays, Patrick D. Miller, and Paul J. Achtemeier. Atlanta: John Knox, 1985.

——. "Praying Through Clenched Teeth." In *The Twentieth Century Pulpit,* vol. 2, edited by James W. Cox with Patricia Parrent Cox. Nashville: Abingdon, 1981.

——. *Preaching.* Nashville: Abingdon, 1985.

——. "Preaching and the Shock of Recognition." The Hickman Lectures, Duke Divinity School, Durham, NC, October 30, 1984. Cassette.

————. "Recent New Testament Interpretation and Preaching." *Princeton Seminary Bulletin* 66, no. 1 (October 1973): 77-81.

————. "The Sermon and the Use of Scripture." *Theology Today* 42 (April 1985): 7-14.

————. "The Sermon as Twice-told Tale." The Sprunt Lectures, Union Theological Seminary, Richmond, VA, February 4-6, 1991. Cassette.

Crites, Stephen. "The Narrative Quality of Experience." *Journal of the American Academy of Religion* 39, no. 3 (September 1971): 291-310.

Cunningham, Cornelius Carman. *Literature as a Fine Art: Analysis and Interpretation.* New York: Ronald Press, 1941.

————. *Making Words Come Alive: The Art of Oral Interpretation of Literature.* Dubuque: Wm. C. Brown, 1951.

Curry, S. S. *The Province of Expression: A Search for Principles Underlying Adequate Methods of Developing Dramatic and Oratoric Delivery.* Boston: Freeman Place, 1891.

————. *Vocal and Literary Interpretation of the Bible.* Boston: Expression, 1923.

Davies, Horton. *Studies of the Church in History.* Allison Park, PA: Pickwick Publications, 1983.

Davies, Oliver. *A Theology of Compassion.* Grand Rapids: Eerdmans, 2001.

Dawson, Sheila. "'Distancing' as an Aesthetic Principle." *Australasian Journal of Philosophy* 39, no. 2 (August 1961): 155-74.

Day, Dennis. "Persuasion and the Concept of Identification." *Quarterly Journal of Speech* 46, no. 3 (October 1960): 270-73.

De Quincey, Thomas. *Confessions of an English Opium-Eater and Suspiria De Profundis.* Boston: Ticknor, Reed, and Fields, 1851.

Dickie, George. *Aesthetics.* New York: Bobbs-Merrill, 1977.

————. *Aesthetics: An Introduction.* New York: Bobbs-Merrill, 1971.

————. "All Aesthetic Attitude Theories Fail: The Myth of the Aesthetic Attitude." In *Aesthetics: A Critical Anthology,* edited by George Dickie, Richard Scalfani, and Ronald Roblin. New York: St. Martin's Press, 1989.

————. *Art and Aesthetic: An Institutional Analysis.* Ithaca: Cornell University Press, 1974.

Dingemans, Gijsbert D. J. "A Hearer in the Pew: Homiletical Reflections and Suggestions." In *Preaching as a Theological Task: World, Gospel, Scripture,* Essays in Honor of David Buttrick, edited by Thomas G. Long and Edward Farley. Louisville: Westminster John Knox, 1996.

Dittes, James E. *When the People Say No: Conflict and the Call to Ministry.* San Francisco: Harper and Row, 1979.

Dunning, Stephen. "Exploring a Poem." In *Transactions with Literature: A Fifty-Year Perspective,* edited by Edmund J. Farrell and James R. Squire. Urbana, IL: National Council of Teachers of English, 1990.

Eagleton, Terry. *Literary Theory.* Minneapolis: University of Minnesota Press, 2008.

Ebeling, Gerhard. *Luther: An Introduction to His Thought.* Philadelphia: Fortress, 1972.

———. *Word and Faith.* London: SCM Press, 1963.

Ellingsen, Mark. "Designing the Biblical Narrative Sermon." *Preaching* 6 (May-June 1991): 31-43.

———. *Doctrine and Word: Theology in the Pulpit.* Atlanta: John Knox, 1983.

———. *The Integrity of Biblical Narrative: Story in Theology and Proclamation.* Minneapolis: Fortress, 1990.

———. *Preparation and Manifestation: Sermons for Lent and Easter.* Lima, OH: C.S.S. Publishing, 1992.

Eslinger, Richard L., ed. *Intersections: Post-critical Studies in Preaching.* Grand Rapids: Eerdmans, 1994.

———. *A New Hearing: Living Options in Homiletic Method.* Nashville: Abingdon, 1987.

———. "Story and Image in Sermon Illustration." *Journal for Preachers* 9, no. 2 (Lent 1986): 19-29.

———. *The Web of Preaching: New Options in Homiletic Method.* Nashville: Abingdon, 2002.

Ewen, Frederic. *Bertolt Brecht: His Life, His Art, and His Times.* New York: Citadel Press, 1967.

Eyre, Richard, and Nicholas Wright. *Changing Stages: A View of British and American Theatre in the Twentieth Century.* New York: Knopf, 2001.

Farmer, Herbert H. *Servant of the Word.* Philadelphia: Fortress, 1964.

Farrell, Edmund J., and James R. Squire, eds. *Transactions with Literature: A Fifty-Year Perspective.* For Louise M. Rosenblatt. Urbana, IL: National Council of Teachers of English, 1990.

Finnegan, Ruth. *Oral Poetry: Its Nature, Significance and Social Context.* Cambridge: Cambridge University Press, 1977.

Fish, Stanley E. "Rhetoric." In *Critical Terms for Literary Study,* edited by Frank Lentricchia and Thomas McLaughlin. Chicago: University of Chicago Press, 1990.

———. *Self-Consuming Artifacts: The Experience of Seventeenth-Century Literature.* Berkeley: University of California Press, 1972.

Ford, David. "System, Story, Performance: A Proposal About the Role of Narrative in Christian Systematic Theology." In *Why Narrative? Readings in Narrative Theology,* edited by Stanley Hauerwas and L. Gregory Jones. Grand Rapids: Eerdmans, 1989.

Frei, Hans W. *The Eclipse of Biblical Narrative: A Study of Eighteenth and Nineteenth Century Hermeneutics.* New Haven, CT: Yale University Press, 1974.

———. *The Identity of Jesus Christ: The Hermeneutical Bases of Dogmatic Theology.* Philadelphia: Fortress, 1975.

————. *Theology and Narrative: Selected Essays*. Edited by George Hunsinger and William C. Placher. New York: Oxford University Press, 1993.

————. *Types of Christian Theology*. Edited by George Hunsinger and William C. Placher. New Haven: Yale University Press, 1992.

Funk, Robert, ed. *Language, Hermeneutic and the Word of God: The Problem of Language in the New Testament and Contemporary Theology*. New York: Harper and Row, 1966.

Gadamer, Hans-Georg. *Philosophical Hermeneutics*. Translated and edited by David E. Linge. Berkeley: University of California Press, 1976.

————. *Truth and Method*. New York: Crossroad Publishing, 1984.

————. "The Universality of the Hermeneutical Problem." In *Art and Interpretation: An Anthology of Readings in Aesthetics and the Philosophy of Art*, edited by Eric Dayton. Toronto, Ontario: Broadview Press, 1998.

Geertz, Clifford. "From a Native's Point of View." In *Interpretive Social Science: A Reader*, edited by Paul Rabinow and William M. Sullivan. Berkeley: University of California Press, 1979.

————. *The Interpretation of Cultures*. New York: Basic Books, 1973.

Geiger, Don. *The Sound, Sense, and Performance of Literature*. Glenview, IL: Scott, Foresman, 1963.

Gentile, John S. *Cast of One: One-Person Shows from the Chautauqua Platform to the Broadway Stage*. Urbana, IL: University of Illinois Press, 1989.

Gerrish, Brian A. Review of *The Nature of Doctrine: Religion and Theology in a Post-liberal Age*, by George A. Lindbeck. *Journal of Religion* 68 (January 1998): 87-92.

Gibson, Andrew. *Towards a Postmodern Theory of Narrative*. Edinburgh: Edinburgh University Press, 1996.

Gilbert, Katharine Everett, and Helmut Kuhn. *A History of Esthetics*. Bloomington: Indiana University Press, 1954.

Goldberg, Michael. *Theology and Narrative: A Critical Introduction*. Philadelphia: Trinity Press International, 1991.

Gottlieb, Marvin R. *Oral Interpretation*. New York: McGraw-Hill, 1980.

Graham, Gordon. *Philosophy of the Arts: An Introduction to Aesthetics*. New York: Routledge, 2005.

————. *The Re-enchantment of the World: Art verses Religion*. New York: Oxford University Press, 2007.

Gray, Giles Wilkeson. "What Was Elocution?" *Quarterly Journal of Speech* 46, no. 1 (February 1960): 1-7.

Green, Garrett, ed. *Scriptural Authority and Narrative Interpretation*. Philadelphia: Fortress, 1987.

Greenhaw, David. "As One *With* Authority: Rehabilitating Concepts for Preaching." In *Intersections: Post-Critical Studies in Preaching*, edited by Richard Eslinger. Grand Rapids: Eerdmans, 1994.

Grondin, Jean. "Hermeneutics and Relativism." In *Festivals of Interpretation: Es-*

says on Hans-Georg Gadamer's Work, edited by Kathleen Wright. Albany: State University of New York Press, 1990.

Grotowski, Jerzy. *Towards a Poor Theatre*. New York: Simon and Schuster, 1968.

Gustafson, James M. "Just What is 'Postliberal' Theology?" *Christian Century* 116 (March 24, 1999): 353-55.

————. "Liberal Questions: A Response to William Placher." *Christian Century* 116 (April 14, 1999): 422-25.

Haas, Richard, and David A. Williams. *The Study of Oral Interpretation: Theory and Comment*. Indianapolis: Bobbs-Merrill, 1975.

Harari, Josué, ed. *Textual Strategies: Perspectives in Post-Structuralist Criticism*. Ithaca: Cornell University Press, 1979.

Harris, Max. *Theatre and Incarnation*. London: Macmillan Press, 1990.

Hauerwas, Stanley, Richard Bondi, and David B. Burrell. *Truthfulness and Tragedy: Further Investigations in Christian Ethics*. Notre Dame, IN: University of Notre Dame Press, 1977.

Hauerwas, Stanley, and L. Gregory Jones, eds. *Why Narrative? Readings in Narrative Theology*. Grand Rapids: Eerdmans, 1989.

Heston, Lilla. "Performing the Modern Novel." Lecture presented at The School of Speech, Northwestern University, Evanston, IL, 1983.

Hilkert, Mary Catherine, O.P. "Revelation and Proclamation: Shifting Paradigms." In *In the Company of Preachers*, edited by the faculty of the Aquinas Institute of Theology. Collegeville, MN: Liturgical Press, 2002.

————. Review of *Preaching Jesus: New Directions for Homiletics in Hans Frei's Postliberal Theology*, by Charles Lamar Campbell. *Worship* 72 (September 1998): 464-65.

Hillman, James. *Insearch: Psychology and Religion*. Woodstock, CN: Spring Publications, 1994.

Hodgson, Peter. *Jesus — Word and Presence*. Philadelphia: Fortress, 1971.

Hogan, Lucy Lind. *Graceful Speech: An Invitation to Preaching*. Louisville: Westminster John Knox, 2006.

Hogan, Lucy Lind, and Robert Reid. *Connecting Congregation: Rhetoric and the Art of Preaching*. Nashville: Abingdon Press, 1999.

Holman, C. Hugh, ed. *Handbook to Literature*. Bobbs-Merrill Educational Publishing, 1980.

Holmes, Arthur B. "Parable as the Form of the Language of Jesus Which Corresponds to the Incarnation." *Drew Gateway* 48, no. 2 (1977): 15-25.

Hooke, Ruthanna. "'I Am Here in This Room . . .' The Practice of Performance and the Learning of Preaching." *Homiletic* 27, no. 1 (Summer 2002): 13-21.

Howell, Wilbur Samuel. "Sources of the Elocutionary Movement in England, 1700-1748." *Quarterly Journal of Speech* 45 (1959): 1-18.

Hughes, Donald E. "Socrates and the Rhapsode: Plato's Ion." In *Studies in Interpre-*

tation, vol. 2, edited by Esther M. Doyle and Virginia Hasting Floyd. Amsterdam: Editions Rodopi N.V., 1977.

Janaway, Christopher. "Aesthetic Attitude" and "Aesthetic Distance." In *The Oxford Companion to Philosophy*, edited by Ted Honderich. Oxford: Oxford University Press, 1995.

Jensen, Richard. *Thinking in Story: Preaching in a Post-Literate Age.* Lima, OH: C.S.S. Publishing, 1993.

Kant, Immanuel. *The Critique of Judgment.* Translated by Werner S. Pluhar. Indianapolis: Hackett, 1987.

————. "A Theory of Esthetic Experience." In *A Modern Book of Esthetics*, edited by Melvin Rader. New York: Holt, Rinehart, and Winston, 1979.

Kay, James F. *Christus Praesens: A Reconsideration of Rudolf Bultmann's Christology.* Grand Rapids: Eerdmans, 1994.

————. *Preaching and Theology.* St. Louis: Chalice Press, 2007.

————. Review of *The Integrity of Biblical Narrative: Story in Theology and Proclamation*, by Mark Ellingsen. *Princeton Seminary Bulletin* 13, no. 3 (1992): 365-66.

————. Review of *Preaching Jesus: New Directions for Homiletics in Hans Frei's Postliberal Theology*, by Charles Lamar Campbell. *Theology Today* 56 (October 1999): 403-5.

————. "Theological Table Talk: Myth or Narrative? Bultmann's 'New Testament and Mythology' Turns Fifty." *Theology Today* 48 (October 1991): 326-32.

Kaye, Nick. *Postmodernism and Performance.* London: Macmillan Press, 1994.

Keck, Leander E. Review of *The Eclipse of Biblical Narrative: A Study in Eighteenth and Nineteenth Century Hermeneutics*, by Hans W. Frei. *Theology Today* 31, no. 4 (January 1975): 367-70.

Kierkegaard, Søren. *Attack Upon "Christendom."* Translated by Walter Lowrie. Princeton, NJ: Princeton University Press, 1944.

————. *Concluding Unscientific Postscript.* Translated by David Swenson and Walter Lowrie. Princeton, NJ: Princeton University Press, 1941.

————. *The Point of View for My Work as an Author: A Report to History.* Translated by Walter Lowrie. New York: Harper and Row, 1962.

Kleinau, Marion L., and Janet Larsen McHughes. *Theatres for Literature: A Practical Aesthetics for Group Interpretation.* Sherman Oaks, CA: Alfred Publishing, 1980.

Kolesnikoff, Nina. "Defamilarization." *Encyclopedia of Contemporary Literary Theory*, edited by Irena R. Makaryk. Toronto: University of Toronto Press, 1993.

Krondorfer, Björn, ed. *Body and Bible: Interpreting and Experiencing Biblical Narratives.* Philadelphia: Trinity Press International, 1992.

Langer, Susanne K. *Feeling and Form: A Theory of Art, Developed from Philosophy in a New Key.* New York: Scribner, 1953.

————. *Philosophy in a New Key: A Study in the Symbolism of Reason, Rite, and Art.* Cambridge, MA: Harvard University Press, 1979.

Langfield, Herbert Sidney. *The Aesthetic Attitude.* New York: Harcourt, Brace, 1920.

Lee, Charlotte I. *Oral Interpretation*. Cambridge, MA: Riverside Press, 1959.

Lee, Charlotte I., and Frank Galati. *Oral Interpretation*. New York: Holt, Rinehart, and Winston, 1977.

Lentricchia, Frank. *After the New Criticism*. Chicago: University of Chicago Press, 1980.

Lentricchia, Frank, and Thomas McLaughlin, eds. *Critical Terms for Literary Study*. Chicago: University of Chicago Press, 1990.

Lindbeck, George A. "The Bible as Realistic Narrative." *Journal of Ecumenical Studies* 17, no. 1 (Winter 1980): 81-85.

———. *The Nature of Doctrine: Religion and Theology in a Postliberal Age*. Philadelphia: Westminster Press, 1984.

Lipps, Theodor. "Empathy, Inner Imitation, and Sense-Feeling." In *A Modern Book of Esthetics*, edited by Melvin Rader. New York: Holt, Rinehart, and Winston, 1979.

Lischer, Richard. "The Limits of Story." *Interpretation* 38, no. 1 (January 1984): 26-39.

———. "Preaching and the Rhetoric of Promise." *Word and World* 8, no. 1 (1988): 66-79.

———. *A Theology of Preaching: The Dynamics of the Gospel*. Durham, NC: Labyrinth Press, 1992.

———. *Theories of Preaching: Selected Readings in the Homiletical Tradition*. Durham, NC: Labyrinth Press, 1987.

Listowel, the Earl of. *Modern Aesthetics: An Historical Introduction*. New York: Teachers College Press, 1967.

Livio, Norma J., and Sandra A. Rietz. *Storytelling: Process and Practice*. Littleton, CO: Libraries Unlimited, 1986.

Long, Beverly Whitaker. "A 'Distanced' Art: Interpretation at Mid-Century." In *Performance of Literature in Historical Perspectives*, edited by David W. Thompson. Lanham, MD: University Press of America, 1983.

———. "Evaluating Performed Literature." In *Studies in Interpretation*, vol. 2, edited by Esther M. Doyle and Virginia Hasting Floyd. Amsterdam: Editions Rodopi N.V., 1977.

Long, Beverly Whitaker, and Mary Frances Hopkins. *Performing Literature: An Introduction to Oral Interpretation*. Englewood Cliffs, NJ: Prentice Hall, 1982.

Long, Thomas G. *The Witness of Preaching*. Louisville: Westminster John Knox, 1989.

———. "And How Shall They Hear? The Listener in Contemporary Preaching." In *Listening to the Word: Studies in Honor of Fred B. Craddock*, edited by Gail R. O'Day and Thomas G. Long. Nashville: Abingdon, 1993.

Longinus. "On the Sublime." In *Critical Theory Since Plato*, edited by Hazard Adams. New York: Harcourt Brace Jovanovich, 1992.

Lord, Albert B. *The Singer of Tales*. 1960. Reprint, New York: Atheneum, 1978.

Lose, David J. "Narrative and Proclamation in a Postliberal Homiletic." *Homiletic* 23, no. 1 (Summer 1998): 1-14.

————. Review of *Preaching Jesus: New Directions for Homiletics in Hans Frei's Postliberal Theology*, by Charles Lamar Campbell. *Currents in Theology and Mission* 25 (August 1998): 322-23.

Lowry, Eugene L. *The Homiletical Plot: The Sermon as Narrative Art Form*. Atlanta: John Knox Press, 1989.

————. *The Homiletical Plot: The Sermon as Narrative Art Form*. Louisville: Westminster John Knox Press, 2001.

————. *How to Preach a Parable: Designs for Narrative Sermons*. Nashville: Abingdon, 1989.

————. "The Revolution of Sermonic Shape." In *Listening to the Word: Studies in Honor of Fred B. Craddock*, edited by Gail R. O'Day and Thomas G. Long. Nashville: Abingdon, 1993.

Lyons, Mary E. "Style." In *Concise Encyclopedia of Preaching*, edited by William H. Willimon and Richard Lischer. Louisville: Westminster John Knox, 1995.

Mackey, Louis. *Kierkegaard: A Kind of Poet*. Philadelphia: University of Pennsylvania Press, 1971.

Maclay, Joanna H. *Readers Theatre: Toward a Grammar of Practice*. New York: Random House, 1971.

Maclay, Joanna H., and Thomas O. Sloan. *Interpretation: An Approach to the Study of Literature*. New York: Random House, 1972.

Margolis, Joseph, ed. *Philosophy Looks at the Arts: Contemporary Readings in Aesthetics*. Philadelphia: Temple University Press, 1987.

Martin, Wallace. *Recent Theories of Narrative*. Ithaca: Cornell University Press, 1986.

McClure, John S. "Narrative and Preaching: Sorting It All Out." *Journal for Preachers* 15, no. 1 (Advent 1991): 24-29.

————. Review of *Preaching Jesus: New Directions for Homiletics in Hans Frei's Postliberal Theology*, by Charles L. Campbell. *Journal for Preachers* 21, no. 2 (1998): 35-37.

Mitchell, Henry H. *Celebration and Experience in Preaching*. Nashville: Abingdon, 1990.

————. *The Recovery of Preaching*. New York: Harper and Row, 1977.

Mitchell, W. J. T., ed. *On Narrative*. Chicago: University of Chicago Press, 1980.

Morrison, Karl F. *"I Am You." The Hermeneutics of Empathy in Western Literature, Theology, and Art*. Princeton, NJ: Princeton University Press, 1988.

Mueller-Vollmer, Kurt, ed. *The Hermeneutics Reader*. New York: Continuum Publishing, 1994.

Murphy, James J. "Saint Augustine and the Debate About a Christian Rhetoric." *Quarterly Journal of Speech* 46, no. 4 (December 1960): 400-410.

O'Day, Gail R., and Thomas G. Long, eds. *Listening to the Word*. Nashville: Abingdon, 1993.

Ong, Walter J., S.J. *Orality and Literacy: The Technologizing of the Word*. New York: Routledge, 1982.

———. *The Presence of the Word: Some Prolegomena for Cultural and Religious History*. Minneapolis: University of Minnesota Press, 1981.

Ortega y Gasset, José. *The Dehumanization of Art*. Princeton, NJ: Princeton University Press, 1948.

———. "The Dehumanization of Art." In *A Modern Book of Esthetics*, edited by Melvin Rader. New York: Holt, Rinehart, and Winston, 1979.

Osborn, Robert T. "A New Hermeneutic?" *Interpretation* 20 (October 1966): 400-411.

Palmer, Richard E. *Hermeneutics*. Evanston, IL: Northwestern University Press, 1969.

Pandit, Sueh. "In Defense of Psychical Distance." *British Journal of Aesthetics* 16, no. 1 (Winter 1976): 56-60.

Pavis, Patrice. *Theatre at the Crossroads of Culture*. Translated by Loren Kruger. London: Routledge, 1992.

Pelias, Ronald J. *Performance Studies: The Interpretation of Aesthetic Texts*. New York: St. Martin's Press, 1992.

———. *Writing Performance: Poeticizing the Researcher's Body*. Carbondale, IL: Southern Illinois University Press, 1999.

Pelias, Ronald J., and James VanOosting. "A Paradigm for Performance Studies." *Quarterly Journal of Speech* 73 (1987): 219-31.

Perkins, William. *The Art of Prophesying with The Calling of Ministry*. 1607. Reprint, Edinburgh: Banner of Truth Trust, 1996.

Phelan, Peggy, and Jill Lane, eds. *The Ends of Performance*. New York: New York University Press, 1998.

Pipa, Joseph A. Jr. "William Perkins and the Development of Puritan Preaching." PhD diss., Westminster Theological Seminary, 1985. Text-fiche.

Placher, William C. "Being Postliberal: A Response to James Gustafson." *Christian Century* (April 7, 1999): 390-93.

———. Introduction to Hans W. Frei, *Theology and Narrative: Selected Essays*, edited by George Hunsinger and William C. Placher. New York: Oxford University Press, 1993.

Plato. "Ion." In *Critical Theory Since Plato*, edited by Hazard Adams. New York: Harcourt Brace Jovanovich, 1992.

Pollock, Della, ed. *Exceptional Spaces: Essays in Performance and History*. Chapel Hill: University of North Carolina Press, 1998.

———. "Performing Writing." In *The Ends of Performance*, edited by Peggy Phelan and Jill Lane. New York: New York University Press, 1998.

Powell, Mark Allan. *What Is Narrative Criticism?* Minneapolis: Fortress Press, 1991.

Presbyterian Hymnal: Hymns, Psalms, and Spiritual Songs. Louisville: Westminster John Knox, 1990.

Prickett, Stephen. *Words and The Word: Language, Poetics and Biblical Interpretation.* Cambridge: Cambridge University Press, 1986.

Prince, Gerald. "Introduction to the Study of the Narratee." In *Reader-Response Criticism: From Formalism to Post-Structuralism,* edited by Jane P. Tompkins. Baltimore: Johns Hopkins University Press, 1980.

Quinn, Edward. *Literary and Thematic Terms.* New York: Checkmark Books, 2000.

Rader, Melvin. "The Meaning of Art." In *A Modern Book of Esthetics,* edited by Melvin Rader. New York: Holt, Rinehart, and Winston, 1979.

Randolph, David James. Introduction to *On Prayer: Nine Sermons by Gerhard Ebeling.* Translated by James W. Leitch. Philadelphia: Fortress, 1967.

———. *The Renewal of Preaching.* Philadelphia: Fortress, 1969.

Rice, Charles. *The Embodied Word: Preaching as Art and Liturgy.* Minneapolis: Fortress, 1991.

———. *Interpretation and Imagination: The Preacher and Contemporary Literature.* Philadelphia: Preacher's Paperback Library, Fortress Press, 1970.

Richards, I. A. *Principles of Literary Criticism.* New York: Harcourt, Brace and World, 1925.

Ricoeur, Paul. "Biblical Hermeneutics." *Semeia* 4 (1975): 29-148.

———. "The Hermeneutical Function of Distanciation." In *Hermeneutics and the Human Sciences: Essays on Language, Action, and Interpretation.* Translated and edited by John B. Thompson. New York: Cambridge University Press, 1994.

———. *Interpretation Theory: Discourse and the Surplus of Meaning.* Fort Worth: Texas Christian University Press, 1976.

Robinson, James, and John Cobb, eds. *The New Hermeneutic.* New Frontiers in Theology, vol. 2. New York: Harper and Row, 1964.

Robinson, Wayne Bradley, ed. *Journeys Toward Narrative Preaching.* New York: Pilgrim Press, 1990.

Rodenberg, Patsy. *The Need for Words: Voice and Text.* London: Methuen Drama, 1993.

Roloff, Leland H. *The Perception and Evocation of Literature.* Glenview, IL: Scott, Foresman, 1973.

Rose, Lucy Atkinson. *Sharing the Word: Preaching in the Roundtable Church.* Louisville: Westminster John Knox, 1996.

Rosenblatt, Louise M. "Act 1, Scene 1: Enter the Reader." *Literature in Performance* 1, no. 2 (1981): 13-23.

———. *Literature as Exploration.* New York: Noble and Noble, 1976.

———. *Literature as Exploration.* New York: Modern Language Association of America, 1991.

———. *The Reader, the Text, the Poem: The Transactional Theory of the Literary Work.* Carbondale, IL: Southern Illinois University Press, 1978.

————. "Reaffirming *Literature as Exploration*." In *Transactions with Literature: A Fifty-Year Perspective*, for Louise M. Rosenblatt, edited by Edmund J. Farrell and James R. Squire. Urbana: National Council of Teachers of English, 1990.

————. "Retrospect." In *Transactions with Literature: A Fifty-Year Perspective*, for Louise M. Rosenblatt, edited by Edmund J. Farrell and James R. Squire. Urbana: National Council of Teachers of English, 1990.

Said, Edward. "Text, The World, The Critic." In *Textual Strategies: Perspectives in Post-Structuralist Criticism*, edited by Josué Harari. Ithaca, NY: Cornell University Press, 1979.

Sauter, Gerhard, and John Barton, eds. *Revelation and Story: Narrative Theology and the Centrality of Story.* Aldershot, UK: Ashgate, 2000.

Sayre, Henry. "Performance." In *Critical Terms for Literary Study*, edited by Frank Lentricchia and Thomas McLaughlin. Chicago: University of Chicago Press, 1990.

Schechner, Richard. *Essays on Performance Theory, 1970-1976.* New York: Drama Book Specialists, 1977.

————. *Performance Theory.* New York: Routledge, 1988.

————. "What Is Performance Studies Anyway?" In *The Ends of Performance*, edited by Peggy Phelan and Jill Lane. New York: New York University Press, 1998.

Schiller, Jerome P. *I. A. Richards' Theory of Literature.* New Haven: Yale University Press, 1969.

Schmit, Clayton J. *Too Deep for Words: A Theology of Liturgical Expression.* Louisville: Westminster John Knox, 2002.

Schner, George P. "*The Eclipse of Biblical Narrative:* Analysis and Critique." *Modern Theology* 8, no. 2 (April 1992): 149-72.

Simmons, Martha F., ed. *Preaching on the Brink: The Future of Homiletics.* Nashville: Abingdon, 1996.

Sittler, Joseph. "The Role of the Imagination." In *Theories of Preaching: Selected Readings in the Homiletical Tradition*, edited by Richard Lischer. Durham, NC: Labyrinth Press, 1987.

Postema, Don. *Space for God.* Grand Rapids: CRC Publications, 1983.

Stanislavski, Constantine. *An Actor's Handbook.* Translated and edited by Elizabeth Reynolds Hapgood. New York: Theatre Arts Books, 1963.

Steimle, Edmund A., Morris J. Niedenthal, and Charles L. Rice. *Preaching the Story.* Philadelphia: Fortress, 1983.

Stern, Carol Simpson, and Bruce Henderson. *Performance: Texts and Contexts.* White Plains, NY: Longman Publishing, 1993.

Stolnitz, Jerome. *Aesthetics.* New York: Macmillan, 1965.

————. *Aesthetics and Philosophy of Art Criticism: A Critical Introduction.* Boston: Houghton Mifflin, 1960.

Taylor, Mark Lewis. Interview by author. Princeton Theological Seminary, Princeton, NJ, 2003.

Thiemann, Ronald F. "Response to George Lindbeck." *Theology Today* 43, no. 3 (October 1986): 377-82.

Thiselton, Anthony C. *The Two Horizons: New Testament Hermeneutics and Philosophical Description.* Grand Rapids: Eerdmans, 1984.

Thompson, David W., ed. *Performance of Literature in Historical Perspectives.* Lanham, MD: University Press of America, 1983.

"Thornton Wilder Credits on Broadway." Internet Broadway Database: http://www.idbd.com (accessed January 2003).

Thornton Wilder Society: http://www.thorntonwildersociety.com (accessed January 2003).

Tisdale, Leonora Tubbs. *Preaching as Local Theology and Folk Art.* Minneapolis: Fortress, 1997.

———. Interview by author. Princeton Theological Seminary, Princeton, NJ, 1997.

Tompkins, Jane P., ed. *Reader-Response Criticism: From Formalism to Post-Structuralism.* Baltimore: Johns Hopkins University Press, 1980.

Turko, Lewis. *The Book of Literary Terms: The Genres of Fiction, Drama, Nonfiction, Literary Criticism, and Scholarship.* Hanover, NH: University Press of New England, 1999.

Turner, Victor. *The Anthropology of Performance.* New York: PAJ Publications, 1986.

———. *From Ritual to Theatre: The Human Seriousness of Play.* New York: PAJ Publications, 1982.

———. "Social Dramas and Stories about Them." In *On Narrative,* edited by W. J. T. Mitchell. Chicago: University of Chicago Press, 1980.

Vaughn, Jack A. *Drama A to Z.* New York: Frederick Ungar Publishing, 1978.

Ward, Richard F. "A New Look at an Ancient Practice: Public Reading in a Plugged In Church." *Papers of the Annual Meeting.* Academy of Homiletics, 35th Meeting (2000): 117-27.

———. "Performance Turns in Homiletics: Wrong Way or Right On?" *Journal of Communication and Religion* 17, no. 1 (March 1994): 1-11.

———. *Speaking from the Heart: Preaching with Passion.* Nashville: Abingdon, 1992.

Weeden, Theodore. *Mark: Traditions in Conflict.* Philadelphia: Fortress, 1979.

Weitz, Morris, ed. *Problems in Aesthetics: An Introductory Book of Readings.* London: Macmillan, 1970.

———. "The Role of Theory in Aesthetics." In *A Modern Book of Esthetics,* edited by Melvin Rader. New York: Holt, Rinehart, and Winston, 1979.

Wheelwright, Philip. *The Burning Fountain: A Study in the Language of Symbolism.* Bloomington: Indiana University Press, 1968.

———. *Metaphor and Reality.* Bloomington: Indiana University Press, 1968.

White, Hayden. "The Metaphysics of Narrativity: Time and Symbol in Ricoeur's Philosophy of History." In *On Paul Ricoeur: Narrative and Interpretation,* edited by David Wood. New York: Routledge, 1991.

———. "The Value of Narrativity in the Representation of Reality." In *On Narrative*, edited by W. J. T. Mitchell. Chicago: University of Chicago Press, 1980.

Whitmore, Jon. *Directing Postmodern Theater: Shaping Signification in Performance.* Ann Arbor: University of Michigan Press, 1994.

Wicker, Brian. *The Story-Shaped World: Fiction and Metaphysics; Some Variations on a Theme.* Notre Dame, IN: University of Notre Dame Press, 1975.

Wilder, Amos. *The Language of the Gospel.* Cambridge, MA: Harvard University Press, 1970.

———. "The Word as Address and the Word as Meaning." In *The New Hermeneutic*, edited by James Robinson and John Cobb. New Frontiers in Theology, vol. 2. New York: Harper and Row, 1964.

Wilder, Thornton. Preface to *Three Plays by Thornton Wilder: Our Town, The Skin of Our Teeth, The Matchmaker.* New York: Bantam Books, 1961.

Willimon, William H., and Richard Lischer, eds. *Concise Encyclopedia of Preaching.* Louisville: Westminster John Knox, 1995.

Wimsatt, W. K., and Monroe C. Beardsley. "The Intentional Fallacy." In *Critical Theory Since Plato*, edited by Hazard Adams. New York: Harcourt Brace Jovanovich, 1992.

Wood, David, ed. *On Paul Ricoeur: Narrative and Interpretation.* New York: Routledge, 1991.

Wuthnow, Robert. *After the Baby Boomers.* Princeton, NJ: Princeton University Press, 2007.

Yale Bulletin and Calendar News Stories: http://www.yale.edu (accessed March 2012).

Yale Repertory Theatre: http://www.yale.edu (accessed February 2012).

Yordon, Judy E. *Roles in Interpretation.* Madison, WI: William C. Brown and Benchmark Publishers, 1993.

Index

Abrams, M. H., 13, 22
Absorption, 120; use of by Auerbach, 133-35; use of by Campbell, 131, 133; use of by Ellingsen, 131, 133; use of by Frei, 133; use of by Lindbeck, 133
Aesthetic (adj.), 12; use of by philosophers or theorists, 12
Aesthetic attitude, 12
Aesthetic distance, 12
Aesthetic experience, 12
Aesthetics, 11-12
Aisthēsis (Greek: "sense perception" or "sensory cognition"), 11
Alienation devices, use of by Brecht, 9, 17n15, 35, 36-38, 46, 144
Allison, Henry E., 13n8
Aristotle, 28
Art of Prophesying, The (Perkins), 49, 125
Ascriptive logic, 97, 121-22, 123, 124, 127-28
Auerbach, Erich, 92, 102-3; use of absorption (or "lure"), 133-35
Austen, Jane, 40

Bacon, Wallace, 23, 24, 25, 25n32, 26, 27, 28, 31n46, 45; dangerous shores

metaphor of, 23, 47; definition of interpretation, 27; on modes, 28-30
Barth, Karl, 55-56, 103
Bartow, Charles L., 3, 22; on body gesture, 83; on elocution, 25; on the sermon as conversation rather than declamation, 142-43, 142n11; on the sermon as a "preaching moment," 85, 85-86n61, 142n11
Baumgarten, Alexander Gottlieb, 11-12
Beardslee, William A., 55, 55n12
Belasco, David, 33
Berleant, Arnold, 42-43, 44n67
Blount, Brian K., 140
Booth, Wayne C., 40
Bozarth-Campbell, Alla, 28
"Bracketing out," 15
Brecht, Bertolt, 9, 55, 87, 144; and epic theater, 36, 36n53, 37n54; and the redirection of theater from being "fun" private entertainment to being "collective creativity," 39; use of alienation devices, 9, 17n15, 35, 36-38, 46, 144
Brueggemann, Walter, 126-31
Bullough, Edward, 9-10, 26, 30, 42,

175

58, 79; critics of, 20-22; on distancing devices, 15, 19-20, 20-21; on "overdistanced" artistic work, 105n24; on psychical Distance, 14-18, 45, 83

Bultmann, Rudolf, 55-56, 124

Buttrick, David, 3, 9; on distance as perspective, 143-44, 143n15

Calvin, John, 140n6

Campbell, Charles Lamar, 4, 63, 89, 136; criticism of contemporary homiletics, 113; criticism of Craddock, 119, 121, 123-24, 137-39, 140-41; criticism of Ellingsen, 121; criticism of Lowry, 121; criticism of Rice, 120; on Frei's sermons, 124-25; use of absorption, 131, 133. *See also* Campbell, Charles Lamar, evaluation of his method according to distance; Campbell, Charles Lamar, homiletic method of; "Pain Turned to Newness" (Brueggemann), evaluation of using Campbell's cultural-linguistic criteria and Craddock's function of distance and its benefits

Campbell, Charles Lamar, evaluation of his method according to distance, 122; sermon form and method, 123-26; sermon model (Brueggemann's "Pain Turned to Newness"), 126-31

Campbell, Charles Lamar, homiletic method of, 112-13, 122; appropriation of the cultural-linguistic model, 118-19; as based on Frei's distinctive approach to biblical narrative and his later move toward a postliberal theology, 113-15, 118, 122; as based on Frei's intratextual communal hermeneutic, 119-20,

122; comparison with Ellingsen's method, 114, 120; preaching and communal performance, 115-18; use of ascriptive logic, 121-22, 123, 124

"Can I Also Be Included?" (Craddock), 60-62

Carroll, Noël, 11, 12, 21

Childers, Jana, 3, 22; on distance and spiritual space, 144-45

Cohen, Ted, 13n8

Coleridge, Samuel Taylor, on the "willing suspension of belief," 32, 77n50

"Control of 'Distance' in Jane Austen's 'Emma'" (Booth), 40

Craddock, Fred B., 3-4, 6-10, 45, 87, 106, 121, 122, 146; on the benefits of distance, 8, 47, 124, 128; criticism of, 89-90; encouraging of preachers to read at least fifteen minutes a day from a variety of literature, especially plays, 52-53; on the goal of distance, 9; on the "nod of recognition," 77; on overhearing (distance and participation), 6-9, 54-55, 62, 71, 72; on the "shock of recognition," 60, 77; sources for his homiletics, 7, 48; use of aesthetic distance, 47. *See also* Craddock, Fred B., on distance in delivery; Craddock, Fred B., on distance in interpretation; Craddock, Fred B., on distance in the sermon; "Pain Turned to Newness" (Brueggemann), evaluation of using Campbell's cultural-linguistic criteria and Craddock's function of distance and its benefits

Craddock, Fred B., on distance in delivery, 79-80; the affect of delivery and the reliance on two uses of a "lure," 79-80; characterization of delivery, 79; and community, 86; distance and body gesture, 83; distance and indirect eye contact, 80-82; distance and voice, 84-86; the effect of delivery, 79; the sermon as a "preaching moment," 85, 85n61

Craddock, Fred B., on distance in interpretation, 65-66; beginning with the hearer, 50-53, 63; Craddock's hermeneutic of distance (protecting the text), 63-65; overhearing an argument or conflict in biblical texts (distance and polemics), 57-58; overhearing biblical characters (distance and identification), 58-63; overhearing the biblical text and the gospel (preserving the message), 54-56

Craddock, Fred B., on distance in the sermon: Christian style (room and space), 74-75; comparison with Ellingsen's method, 108-9; distance as an element of style, 66-69, 67-68n35; distance as overhearing and indirect address, 70-74; effecting a new hearing of a familiar message, 75-79; on "too much distance" in a sermon, 105n24

Critique of Judgment (Kant), 13-14

Crossan, John Dominic, 119

"Dangerous Shores, The: From Elocution to Interpretation" (Bacon), 23, 24, 25, 27; dangerous shores metaphor in, 23

Dawson, Sheila, 18n18

Delsarte, François, 26

De Quincey, Thomas, 7, 48, 75-76, 87

Detachment, 17n15

Dewey, John, 48

Dickie, George, 13, 14, 17n16, 21, 22

Distance: aesthetic distance, 11-12; distance in preaching, 1-2; and participation of the recipient or hearer, 105n24; psychical Distance (Bullough), 13-18

Distance in speech performance. *See* Elocution; Literary criticism, and focus on the reader as performer; Modes; Oral interpretation; Presentational performance

Distancing devices, 45; Bullough on, 15, 19-20, 20-21; use of by Thornton Wilder, 9, 17n15, 35-36, 45-46

Dittes, James E., 62n26

"Doxology" (Craddock), 77-79

Ebeling, Gerhard, 84n59

Ecclesiastes, or, A Discourse concerning the Gift of Preaching (Wilkins), 24

Eclipse of Biblical Narrative, The (Frei), 98, 127

"Efficacy/Ritual" and "Entertainment/Theatre" poles, 39

Eliade, Mircea, 89

Eliot, George, 7

Ellingsen, Mark, 4, 50n7, 89, 113, 128-29, 130; criticism of Craddock, 138; on life stories, 94, 101-2, 108-10; use of absorption, 131, 133; use of a problem/solution structure in his published sermons, 110; use of the tools of New Criticism, 96, 104, 106, 111. *See also* Ellingsen, Mark, evaluation of his method according to distance; Ellingsen, Mark, homiletic method of

Ellingsen, Mark, evaluation of his method according to distance, 104; absorption and community, 111-12; distance and identification with biblical characters, 107-10; distance and New Criticism, 104-6; theory and method, 106-7

Ellingsen, Mark, homiletic method of, 90-93, 119; the Bible as realistic narrative, 93-96; "biblical narrative" approach to preaching, 92; comparison with Campbell's method, 114, 120; comparison with Craddock's method, 108-9; comparison with Lindbeck's method, 111-12; criticism of two functions of allegory in contemporary preaching, 99-100; definition of proclamation, 93; identification with biblical characters through the correspondence of our lives with theirs, 97-102; interpretation of biblical characters from within the text, 96-97; luring the hearer into the biblical world, 102-4; sermon delivery as "speaker oriented," 107n28

Elocutio (Latin), 24, 25

Elocution, 23-26; factors contributing to the demise of, 25-26

Engagement, 21

Epic theater, 36, 36n53

Eslinger, Richard L., 86

"Essay on Elocution" (Mason), 24

Existentialism, 65

Faber, Frederick William, 147

Farmer, Herbert H., 143

Finnegan, Ruth, 135n70

Ford, David, 138n3

Forster, E. M., distinction of between story and plot, 121

Frei, Hans, 4, 88, 89, 92, 98, 99, 114, 122, 127, 136; Campbell's critique of, 116; cultural-linguistic turn of, 132; on "figuration," 98, 98n18; on identity and agency, 96; influence of

Lindbeck on, 114; on the language of the Christian community, 116; Schner's critique of, 115-16; use of absorption, 133; use of ascriptive logic, 97, 121, 123; on what it means to read Scripture as "realistic narrative," 94-95

Fuchs, Ernst, 84n59

Funk, Robert, 7, 65n30, 65n33

Gadamer, Hans-Georg, 48

Galati, Frank, 31n46

Geertz, Clifford, 131-33; on "experience near" and "experience distant" concepts, 132-33

Graham, Gordon, 13n8

Greek theater, 33-34; the chorus, 34; masks, 34, 37; and reenactment, 33-34; the role of the actor as symbolic, 33; the stage, 34

Guyer, Paul, 13n8

Hauerwas, Stanley, 138

Hays, Richard, 126

Heidegger, Martin, 84n59

Henderson, Bruce, 5, 6

Heston, Lilla, 82

Hillman, James, 145

Hodgson, Peter, 65n33

Homer, Auerbach's discussion of, 134-35

Interpretation, 6, 22n26

"Is There Still Room for Rhetoric?" (Craddock), 67-68n35

Jones, L. Gregory, 138

Kant, Immanuel, 42; on disinterested contemplation, 13-14, 45

Käsemann, Ernst, 57

Kay, James F., 106, 107, 126

Kierkegaard, Søren, 7, 48, 70, 74, 77, 85, 87; reflection of on his own communication style, 73; sermon of in *Either/Or*, 73
Kinesthetics, 83
Kohut, Heinz, 132
Küng, Hans, 97

Langer, Susanne K., 14
Lash, Nicholas, on performing the Scriptures, 117
Lee, Charlotte, 31n46
Lewes, George Henry, on the *optique du théâtre* ("theater lens"), 32-33n49
Life stories: Ellingsen on, 94, 101-2, 108-10; function of in sermons, 101-2, 102n21
"Limits of Story, The" (Lischer), 94
Lindbeck, George, 4, 88-89, 92, 95, 119, 120, 122, 127; comparison with Ellingsen's method, 111-12; on the experiential-expressive movement, 89, 113; influence of on Frei, 114; on "intratextuality," 96-97; on typology, 98-99, 98n18; use of absorption, 133; use of ascriptive logic, 97
Lischer, Richard, 48, 94, 118
Literary criticism, and focus on the reader as performer, 40-44
Long, Beverly Whitaker, 14n13, 30-31
Long, Thomas G., 102n21
Lord, Alfred B., 135, 135n70
Lowry, Eugene L., 121
Luther, Martin, 108n29
Lyons, Mary E., 67-68, 67n35, 69; on aims of style, 69; on characteristics of sermon style (figures of speech and figures of thought), 68; definition of sermon style, 67
Lyotard, Jean-François, 132n65

Mason, John, 24
McClure, John S., 139n4
Mimesis: The Representation of Reality in Western Culture (Auerbach), 133-35
Mitchell, Henry H., 49-50
Modes, 28-31; dramatic, 29; epic, 29, 29n42; lyric, 28-29; in Scripture, 29
Molé, François René, 33n49

Narrative theology. *See* Postliberal theology
Nature of Doctrine, The (Lindbeck), 111
New Criticism, 42, 93-94, 114; and the affective fallacy, 42, 94, 105; and the intentional fallacy, 42, 94, 105
New Hermeneutic, 31, 48, 84n59
New Testament interpretation, history-of-religions approach to, 55-56
Northwestern University, The School of Speech, lectures at, 31n46

Oral interpretation, 6, 22n26, 26-28
Ortega y Gasset, José, 20
Otto, Rudolf, 89
Our Town (T. Wilder), 9, 35, 39
"Overhearing the Gospel: The Illusion of Truth without Imagination" (Craddock), 6-9, 48
Overhearing the Gospel (Craddock), 48; discussion of a sermon style that is "fitting" in, 71; subtitle of (*Preaching and Teaching the Faith to Persons Who Have Heard It All Before*), 146; use of the terms "room," "space," "freedom," "lure," and "coercion" in, 74, 74n44

"Pain Turned to Newness" (Brueggemann), evaluation of using Campbell's cultural-linguistic criteria and Craddock's function of distance and its benefits, 126-31, 129n63

Pandit, Sueh, 18n18

Parry, Milman, field research of on Yugoslavian *guslars*, 135n70

Performance, 5; and the Old French *perfournir*, 5

Performance event, 5

Performance studies, 6

Perkins, William, 49, 125

Piscator, Erwin, 36n53

Placher, William C., 89n3

"Poem as Event, The" (Rosenblatt), 42

Positivism, 65

Postliberal theology, 88; use of New Criticism, 112

Preaching (Craddock), order of the chapters in, 50-53

Preaching Jesus: New Directions for Hans Frei's Postliberal Theology (Campbell), limited attention to sermon form, method, and construction in, 123

Preaching Moment, The: A Guide to Sermon Delivery (Bartow), 142n11

Preaching styles: African-American preaching, 72n41; Pentecostal preaching, 72n41; Puritan preaching, 49, 125; white mainline Protestant preaching, 48-49, 71, 71-72n41

Presentational performance, 33-34; in Greek theater, 33-34

Prince, Gerald, on the "narratee," 40-41

Proxemics, 83

"'Psychical Distance' as a Factor in Art and an Aesthetic Principle" (Bullough), 9-10; on distancing devices, 15, 19-20; on psychical Distance, 14-18

"Puritan Plain Style" or "New Reformed Method" preaching, 49, 125

Rader, Melvin, 18n18, 21

Randall, Anna T., 24

Reading: oral reading as "expression," 25n31; reading as performance, 40-44

Recovery of Preaching, The (Mitchell), chapter titles in, 50

Representationalism. *See* Representational performance

Representational performance, 31-33, 34

Rhetoric, traditional components of, 48

Rice, Charles, 120

Ricoeur, Paul, 7, 48; on distanciation, 63-64n28

Robinson, Wayne Bradley, 127

Roloff, Leland H., 45; on modes, 28-29; on performance, 29-30

Rosenblatt, Louise, transactional theory of literature of, 41-45, 46, 54, 106; reading as a "performance" in, 105-6; the role of distance in, 105

Ross, William T., 25

Ryle, Gilbert, 21

Saint Joan of the Stockyards (Brecht), 37-38

Schechner, Richard, 39

Schillebeeckx, Edward, 97

Schleiermacher, Friedrich, 89

Schner, George P., critique of Frei's *The Eclipse of Biblical Narrative*, 115-16

Sermon, 5; components of, 5

Sermon text, 5, 6

Shakespeare, William, 23

Sheridan, Thomas, 24; definition of elocution, 27

Singer of Tales, The (Lord), 135, 135n70
Skin of Our Teeth, The (T. Wilder), 35-36
Stanislavski, Constantine, 32, 37
Stern, Carol Simpson, 5, 6
Stolnitz, Jerome, 12n3
Structuralism, 114

Taylor, Mark Lewis, 132
Text, 5-6
Théâtre Libre (Paris), 33
Tisdale, Leonora Tubbs, 140, 140n6; on "hearer-oriented" sermons, 140n6
Tracy, David, 97
Turner, Victor, 5, 144

Vaughn, Jack A., 31n46

Weeden, Theodore, 58
"We Must Be Blind" (Ellingsen), 102, 128-29, 130; crediting of Frei, Auerbach, and Lindbeck in, 92; summary of his homiletical method in, 90-92
"What About the Weeds?" (Craddock), 76-77
"What Happens When We Can't Believe It?" (Ellingsen), 109
Why Narrative? Readings in Narrative Theology (ed. Hauerwas and Jones), 138
Wilder, Amos, 7, 56, 80
Wilder, Thornton, 37; and the shifting of theater back to ritual, 39; use of distancing devices, 9, 17n15, 35-36, 45-46
Wilkins, John, 24
Wuthnow, Robert, on "tinkering," 141

Yale school. *See* Postliberal theology